BURT FRANKLIN: RESEARCH & SOURCE WORKS SERIES 670
Geography and Discovery 12

A TENTATIVE GUIDE TO HISTORICAL MATERIALS
ON THE SPANISH BORDERLANDS

A TENTATIVE GUIDE TO HISTORICAL MATERIALS ON THE SPANISH BORDERLANDS

By Francis Borgia Steck, O.F.M., Ph.D.

BURT FRANKLIN, NEW YORK

Published by LENOX HILL Pub. & Dist. Co. (Burt Franklin)
235 East 44th St., New York, N.Y. 10017
Originally Published: 1943
Reprinted: 1971
Printed in the U.S.A.

S.B.N.: 8337-33796
Library of Congress Card Catalog No.: 71-143659
Burt Franklin: Research and Source Works Series 670
Geography and Discovery 12

Reprinted from the original edition in the University of Illinois
Library.

FOREWORD

Not only in our institutions of learning but also in our periodical literature, not to speak of study clubs and literary societies, there is manifest an ever-increasing interest in the history of the Spanish Borderlands—from Florida westward along the Gulf coast and the Mexican border to the Pacific slopes of California and Oregon northward as far as Alaska. It stands to reason that these territories, being today part of the United States, constitute an integral part of United States history; wherefore a study of these regions where Spain once held sway should certainly find a place on the class schedule of our high schools and colleges and on the programs of fraternities devoted to the mental improvement of their members. As to public lecturers and writers for popular magazines, it seems that they are beginning to realize that the history of the Spanish Borderlands has a fascination all its own and that, like the directors of schools and literary associations, they would give even greater attention to this history if references to the sources of information were more easily available in our libraries and reading rooms. From the lack of these it follows that college professors and research workers, who happen to be engaged in this field of United States history, are today receiving from interested parties more letters of inquiry than they have time and patience to answer, even if they had a bibliography on the Spanish Borderlands in their files or at their fingers' ends.

It was to meet this manifold demand, that is, to guide teachers, students, writers, lecturers, and librarians to the widely scattered materials dealing with this section of our history, especially in our periodical literature, that I set out to prepare the present guide. As the "Key to Periodicals" shows, I regarded not only strictly scientific magazines of history but also popular publications, notably when the author of the article in question was known to have elsewhere published scientific studies in the field of Spanish-American history. The same holds with regard to books which, though popular in form, were

3

deemed worthy of inclusion by reason of their general accuracy and specific interest. Works embodying the results of excavations by archaeological committees and societies were not included when it was found that they dealt technically with the Indian in pre-historic times. Works of this kind are so numerous and scattered that they might well form the subject matter for a special bibliography. Finally it should be noted here that none of the items embodied in the present guide extend beyond the year 1942. Materials published after December of that year will appear in the supplements I plan to issue from time to time.

Being devoted specifically to the periods when our southern and western borderlands were Spanish possessions, at least by title and for most of the time, the guide comprises the following seven parts: (1) general and comprehensive works, covering either the entire region or some larger section thereof; (2) the half century of discovery and exploration by Spain, from 1513 to 1561; (3) Florida, from 1561 to 1819; (4) Louisiana, from 1763 to 1803; (5) Texas, from 1689 to 1836; (6) New Mexico and Arizona, from 1581 to 1846; (7) California and the Northwest, from 1769 to 1846. For obvious reasons, attention was given also to the adjacent lands of Spain, the history of which is intimately bound up with that of our Spanish Borderlands: Georgia and Carolina in the case of Florida; the trans-Mississippi West in the case of Louisiana, the North-Mexican States in the case of Texas, New Mexico and Arizona; Oregon and Alaska in the case of California.

No one who compiles a bibliography of this kind would venture to claim that the finished product is complete and perfect. My judgment on this or that item as to its historical value is by no means infallible. I am also quite confident that worthwhile books and magazine articles have escaped my notice and that errors will be discovered in the titles and data of books and in the volume and page references to magazine articles. For this reason additions and corrections for a future revised edition of the guide will be infinitely more welcome to the compiler than words of commendation and recognition for the present finished product, in the title of which special emphasis ought to be placed on the word "tentative."

4

In conclusion, I wish to acknowledge my indebtedness to all those who have made the publication of this guide possible. I am thinking here especially of the cheerful and persevering assistance rendered me by my students at the Catholic University of America. To them I am deeply grateful, just as I know they are grateful to me for trying to make the course they followed in the history of the Spanish Borderlands as interesting and profitable as I was able. Equally grateful am I to Rt. Rev. Msgr. Bernard A. McKenna, D.D., LL.D., President of THE AMERICAN CATHOLIC HISTORICAL SOCIETY OF PHILADELPHIA. When no one, perhaps for obvious reasons, cared to publish the guide, it was Msgr. McKenna who generously agreed to give it space as a special publication in the RECORDS. Perhaps the demand for it will not be so limited after all and the sale, when all the parts are published, correspondingly compensative. Anyway, I am happy that the guide will appear in the RECORDS whose sponsors seem to be more than usually interested in promoting a cause such as the present guide represents.

FRANCIS BORGIA STECK.

The Catholic University of America,
Washington, D. C.

Feeling that this work of Dr. Steck is of such great importance and present-day events demands its appearance as soon as possible, Monsignor McKenna has decided to give it now to the public in book form rather than await its appearance later in the American Catholic Historical Society Records.

TABLE OF CONTENTS

KEY TO PERIODICALS

AA ....American Anthropologist. American Anthropological Association, Menasha, Wis.

AaA ....Art and Archaeology. Archaeological Institute of America, Washington, D. C.

ACQR ....American Catholic Quarterly Review. Philadelphia, Pa.

AHR ....American Historical Review. Washington, D. C.

AHSI ....Archivum Historicum Societatis Iesu. Rome, Italy.

AIA ....Archivo Ibero-Americano. Madrid, Spain.

AP ....Arrow Points. Alabama Anthropological Society, Montgomery, Ala.

ArizHR ....Arizona Historical Review. University of Arizona, Tucson, Ariz.

ArkHR ....Arkansas Historical Review. Arkansas Historical Society., Little Rock, Ark.

BM ....Bunker's Monthly. The Magazine of Texas, Fort Worth, Tex.

CanHR ....Canadian Historical Review. University of Toronto, Toronto, Canada.

CHR ....Catholic Historical Review. The American Catholic Historical Association, Washington, D. C.

CHSQ ....California Historical Society Quarterly. San Francisco, Calif.

CM ....Colorado Magazine. State Historical Society of Colorado, Denver, Colo.

CO ....Chronicles of Oklahoma, Oklahoma Historical Society, Oklahoma City, Okla.

CW ....The Catholic World. New York, N. Y.

DH ....Divulgacion Historica. Mexico, D. F.

ER ....Ecclesiastical Review. Philadelphia, Pa.

FCHQ ....Filson Club Historical Quarterly. Filson Club, Louisville, Ky.

FH ....Franciscan Herald. Franciscan Herald Press, Chicago, Ill.

FHSQ ....Florida Historical Society Quarterly. Tallahassee, Fla.

FR ....Fortnightly Review. St. Louis, Mo.

GR ....Geographical Review. American Geographical Society, New York, N. Y.

GHQ ....Georgia Historical Quarterly. Georgia Historical Society, Savannah, Ga.

HAHR ....Hispanic American Historical Review.. Duke University, Durham, N. C.

Hpa ....Hispania. Stanford University, Stanford, Calif.

IAA ....Ibero Amerikanisches Archiv. Berlin, Germany.

IH ....Investigaciones Historicas. Mexico, D. F.

IJHP ....Iowa Journal of History and Politics. State Historical Society of Iowa, Iowa City, Ia.

JAH ....Journal of American History. National Historical Society, New York, N. Y.

JMH ....Journal of Modern History. University of Chicago, Chicago, Ill.

JNH ....Journal of Negro History. Washington, D. C.

Ka ....Kiva. Tucson, Ariz.

LHQ ....Louisiana Historical Quarterly. New Orleans, La.

LofS ....Land of Sunshine. Los Angeles, Calif.

M-A ....Mid-America. Loyola University, Chicago, Ill.

MAH ....Magazine of American History.

ME ....Military Engineer. Washington, D. C.

MHR ....Missouri Historical Review. Columbia, Mo.

MVHR ....Mississippi Valley Historical Review. Cedar Rapids, Ia.

NCHR ....North Carolina Historical Review. North Carolina Historical Commission, Raleigh, N. C.

NDUJ ....North Dakota University Journal. University of North Dakota, University, N. Dak.

NH ....Nebraska History. Nebraska History and Record of Pioneer Days, Lincoln, Neb.

NMHR ....New Mexico Historical Review. University of New Mexico, Albuquerque, N. M.

OHQ ....Oregon Historical Quarterly. Oregon Historical Society, Portland, Ore.

OSFe ....Old Santa Fe. Santa Fe, N. M.

OW ....Out West. Los Angeles, Calif

Pa ....El Palacio. Santa Fe, N. M.

PHR ....Pacific Historical Review. Pacific Coast Branch of the American Historical Association, Glendale, Calif.

PSQ ....Political Science Quarterly. Academy of Political Science, New York, N. Y.

RACHSP ....Records of the American Catholic Historical Society of Philadelphia, Philadelphia, Pa.

RHA ....Revista de la Historia de America. Mexico, D. F.

RLI ....Revista de las Indias. Madrid, Spain.

RSUSCHS ....Records and Studies of the United States Catholic Historical Society. New York, N. Y.

RyF ....Razon y Fe. Madrid, Spain.

SCHGM ....South Carolina Historical and Genealogical Magazine.
South Carolina Historical Society, Charleston, S. C.

SegCIHA ....Segundo Congreso Internacional de Historia de America. Buenos Aires, Argentina.

SHQ ....Southwestern Historical Quarterly. University of
Texas, Austin, Tex.

SR ....Southwest Review. Southern Methodist University,
Dallas, Tex.

SSSQ ....Southwest Social Science Quarterly. Austin, Tex.

StLCHR ....St. Louis Catholic Historical Review. St. Louis, Mo.

TGM ....Texas Geographic Magazine. Austin, Tex.

Th ....Thought. New York, N. Y.

UdeM ....Universidad de Mexico. National University of Mexico, Mexico, D. F.

USCHM ....United States Catholic Historical Magazine.

USNIP ....United States Naval Institute Proceedings. United
States Naval Institute, Annapolis, Md.

WHQ ....Washington Historical Quarterly. Seattle, Wash.

I. GENERAL AND COMPREHENSIVE MATERIALS

Alegre, F. J. Historia de la Compañia de Jesús en Nueva España. 3 vols. Mexico, 1841.

Edition of the Jesuit historian's work published by Carlos María de Bustamante. It was begun by the author's confrère, Francisco Florencia, carrying the history down to the expulsion of the Jesuits from New Spain (1767). A continuation of the work was prepared by José Mariano Dávila y Arrillaga, S.J., in two volumes and published in Puebla in 1888. A new edition of the work appeared in Mexico in 1940. The work is important for the history of the Jesuits in northwestern Mexico and Lower California.

Alessio Robles, C. La región arqueológico de Casas Grandes de Chihuahua. Mexico, 1929. (46 p.)

Alessio Robles, V. Francisco de Urdiñola y el norte de la Nueva España. Mexico, 1931. (333 p.)

Alessio Robles, V. (ed.). Pedro Tamarón y Romeral: Demostración del vastísimo obispado de la Nueva Vizcaya, 1765. Mexico, D. F., 1937. (464 p.)

Takes in Durango, Sinaloa, Sonora, Arizona, New Mexico, Chihuahua, and parts of Texas. A scholarly edition with valuable bibliographical Introduction and abundant notes, together with a rich bibliography and six excellent charts.

Alessio Robles, V. (ed.). Coahuila y Texas en la época colonial. Mexico, 1938. (751 p.)

A magnificent study, heavily documented and enriched with valuable illustrations and charts.

Alessio Robles, V. (ed.). Nicolás de Lafora—Relación del viaje que hizo a los presidios internos situados en la frontera de la América septentrional perteneciente al rey de España con un militar bibliográfico y acotaciones por Vito Alessio Robles. Mexico, D. F., 1939. (335 p.)

A richly annotated edition of the report drawn up by the engineer of the inspection tour which Rubí conducted through section of the Spanish Southwest, 1766-1768.

Arlegui, J. Crónica de la Provincia de N. S. P. S. Francisco de Zacatecas. Mexico, 1851. (488 p.)

Bartram, W. Travels through North and South Carolina, Georgia, East and West Florida, the Cherokee country, the extensive territories of the Muscogules or Creek Confederacy, and the country of the Choctaws. Philadelphia, 1791; London, 1792; Dublin, 1793; Paris, 1799.

Beaumont, Pablo de la P. C. Crónica de la Provincia de los Santos Apóstoles S. Pedro y S. Pablo de Michoacán. 5 vols. Mexico, 1873-1874.

This edition, the best, constitutes volumes XV-XIX of the *Biblioteca Histórica de la Iberia*. Beaumont carried the history of the Province down to the year 1575. It should be used in connection with the first discovery and explorations of New Mexico, especially vols. IV and V.

Bemis, S. F. Pinckney's treaty: a study of America's advantage from Europe's distress, 1783-1800. Baltimore: The Johns Hopkins press, 1926. (421 p.)

The introductory chapter (pp. 1-43) treats the Mississippi question from 1763 to 1783, while the remaining portion of this excellent study deals chiefly with Spanish-American diplomacy from 1783 to 1800. The Spanish and English text of the 1795 San Lorenzo treaty takes up pages 391-411

Bernstein, H. "Spanish influence in the United States: economic aspects." HAHR (1938), 43-65.

Blackmar, F. W. Spanish institutions of the Southwest. New York, 1891. (79 p.)

Bolton, H. E. The Spanish borderlands. New Haven, 1921. (320 p.)

Bolton, H. E. Spanish exploration in the Southwest. 1542-1706—Original narratives of early American history. New York, 1925. (487 p.)

This volume contains, in English translation, the original accounts,

11

with critical introduction and abundant annotations in each case, of the following expeditions: (1) exploration and plans for the settlement of California, (2) exploration and settlement in New Mexico and in adjacent regions, (3) exploration and settlement in Texas, (4) Arizona: the Jesuits in Pimería Alta.

Bolton, H. E. and T. M. Marshall. The colonization of North America, 1492-1783. New York, 1920. (609 p.)

A pioneer textbook, "written from the standpoint of North America as a whole, and giving a more adequate treatment of the colonies of nations other than England and of the English colonies other than the thirteen which revolted" (Preface).

Bolton, H. E. Wider horizons of American history. New York, 1939. (191 p.)

Contains the author's four essays: (1) "The epic of greater America," (2) "Defensive Spanish expansion and the significance of the borderlands," (3) "The mission as a frontier institution in the Spanish-American colonies," (4) "The black robes in New Spain."

Bolton, H. E. "Some materials for Southwestern history in the Archivo General de Mexico." SHQ, VI (1902), 103-112; VII (1903), 196-213.

Bolton, H. E. "Materials for Southwestern history in the Central archives of Mexico." AHR, XIII (1908), 510-527.

Bolton, H. E. "The mission as a frontier institution in the Spanish-American colonies." AHR, XXII (1917), 42-61; also in the author's Wider horizons of American history.

Bolton, H. E. "Defensive Spanish expansion and the significance of the borderlands." The Trans-Mississippi West. Boulder: University of Colorado, 1930; also in the author's Wider horizons of American history.

Bolton, H. E. "The epic of greater America." AHR, XXXVIII (1935), 448-474; also in the author's Wider horizons of American history.

Bolton, H. E. "The Black Robes in New Spain, 1572-1767." CHR, XXI (1936), 257-272; also in the author's Wider horizons of American history.

Brebner, J. B. The explorers of North America, 1492-1806. New York, 1933. (502 p.)

An excellent comprehensive study.

Brittain, A. Discovery and exploration—History of North America series. Philadelphia, 1903. (502 p.)

Brooks, P. C. Diplomacy and the borderlands: The Adams-Onís treaty of 1819. Berkeley: University of California press, 1939. (262 p.)

Deals with the 1819 treaty between Spain and the United States with emphasis on the part played by Spain in the negotiations that resulted in the acquisition of Florida from Spain by purchase.

Brooks, P. C. "Pichardo's treatise and the Adams-Onís treaty." HAHR, XV (1935), 94-99.

Discusses the history and influence of Pichardo's exhaustive study, now available in English in C. W. Hackett's three-volume *Pichardo's Limits of Louisiana and Texas.* (See No. 54.)

Brown, A. The genesis of the United States. 2 vols. New York, 1890. (1157 p.)

Buffinton, A. H. The second hundred years war, 1689-1815. New York, 1929. (114 p.)

Burpee, L. J. The search for the western sea. Toronto, 1908. (651 p.)

Castañeda, C. E. "Pioneers in sackcloth." CHR, XXV (1939), 309-320.

Deals with the missionary activities of Franciscans and Jesuits in the Southwest during the sixteenth century.

Caughey, J. W. History of the Pacific coast. Los Angeles, 1933. (429 p.)

Offers for the first time a comprehensive account of events on the entire Pacific coast of North America.

Chesky, J. "Indian music of the Southwest." Ka, VII (1941), 9-12.

Chittenden, H. M. The American fur trade of the Far West. 3 vols., New York, 1902; 2 vols., New York, 1935. (981 p.)

Clark, D. E. The West in American history. New York, 1937. (682 p.)

Contains a good summary of Spain's role in the trans-Mississippi West.

Cooke, P. St. G. Scenes and adventures in the army. New York, 1857. (432 p.)

The story of the author's career in Kearny's army.

Cooke, P. St. G. The conquest of New Mexico and California. New York, 1878. (307 p.)

Story of the American occupation by one who served as lieutenant-colonel under Kearny.

Crane, V. W. The southern frontier, 1670-1732. Durham, N. C.: Duke University press, 1928. (391 p.)

Curtis, F. S., Jr. "Spanish arms and armor in the Southwest." NMHR, II (1927), 179-187.

Daenell, E. Die Spanier in Nordamerika von 1513-1824. Muenchen, 1911. (247 p.)

A summary interpretative account of Spanish enterprises in North America, covering the entire field and colonial period; based on printed sources, primary and secondary; superseded in some matters by more recent researches and studies.

Fergusson, E. Our Southwest. New York, 1940. (376 p.)

Foik, P. J. "Survey of source materials for the Catholic history of the Southwest." CHR, XV (1929), 275-281.

Foik, P. J. "The martyrs of the Southwest." M-A, XI (1928), 27-55; also Preliminary Studies of the Texas Catholic Historical Society (Austin), I (1929), No. 1, (31 p.)

Foreman, G. Advancing the frontier, 1830-1860. Norman: University of Oklahoma press, 1933. (363 p.)

Foreman, G. Indians and pioneers: the story of the American Southwest before 1830. Norman: University of Oklahoma press, 1937. (300 p.)

Frejes, F. Historia breve de la conquista de los estados independientes del Imperio Mexicano. Mexico, 1839; 2nd ed., Guadalajara, 1878. (277 p.)

Garber, P. N. The Gadsden treaty. Philadelphia: University of Pennsylvania press, 1923. (222 p.)

García Icazbalceta, J. (ed.). "Fragmentos de una historia de la Nueva Galicia, escrita hacia 1650 por el P. Fr. Antonio Tello, de la orden de San Francisco." Colección de documentos para la historia de México (Mexico, 1866), II, 343-438. (See No. 95.)

Gardiner, D. West of the river. New York, 1941. (347 p.)

Deals with the trans-Mississippi West after 1800. "The story of the Spanish [in these regions] omits the constructive work of the brave friars and mission leaders" (AHR, XLVII, 1942, p. 367)—unpardonable, considering the scope of the work and the vast amount of source materials now available.

Greenhow, R. The history of Florida, Louisiana, Texas, and California, and the adjoining countries, including the whole valley of the Mississippi. New York, 1856.

Gregg, J. Commerce of the prairies. 2 vols. Philadelphia, 1855.

Griffin, C. C. The United States and the disruption of the Spanish empire, 1810-1822. New York: Columbia University press, 1937. (315 p.)

A thorough study based on Spanish, French, and English manuscripts, taking in the southern borderlands as part of the Spanish empire.

Gunthorp, M. R. The old mission trail. Caldwell, Idaho, 1940. (146 p.)

Habig, M. Heroes of the Cross. New York, 1939. (175 p.)

"The Franciscan martyrs in North America," the vast majority of whom were active and shed their blood in our Spanish borderlands.

Hackett, C. W. and C. C. Shelby (ed. and trans.) Pichardo's treatise on the limits of Louisiana and Texas. 3 vols. Austin: University of Texas press. 1931, 1934, 1941.

This is "an argumentative and historical treatise with reference to the verification of the true limits of the provinces of Louisiana and Texas; written by Father José Antonio Pichardo, of the congregation of the oratory of San Felipe Neri, to disprove the claim of the United States that Texas was included in the Louisiana purchase of 1803" (sub-title). A work of inestimable value and a lasting credit to the high scholarship of editor and translator, a rich storehouse of bibliographical and historical data.

Hackett, C. W. (ed.) Historical documents relating to New Mexico, Nueva Vizcaya, and approaches thereto, to 1773. 3 vols., Washington, D. C.: Carnegie Institution of Washington, 1923, 1926, 1937.

English translations of documents "collected by Adolph F. A. Bandelier and Fanny R. Bandelier." Each volume is introduced by the editor with a scholarly study: (1) "Expansion of Spain in North America, 1492-1590," pp. 3-28; (2) "Nueva Vizcaya in the seventeenth century," pp. 3-82; (3) "Miscellaneous documents relating primarily to New Mexico in the seventeenth and eighteenth centuries," pp. 3-43.

Hackett, C. W. "The delimitation of political jurisdiction in Spanish-America to 1553." HAHR, I (1918), 40-69.

Hafen, J. R. Western America: The exploration, settlement, development of the region beyond the Mississippi. New York, 1941. (698 p.)

It represents "the first comprehensive survey of the history of the land between the Mississippi River and the Pacific Ocean from the time of Cabeza de Vaca and Coronado to Theodore Roosevelt" (AHR, Jan., 1942, p. 368). Early chapters deal with the Spaniards in our southern borderlands. Useful for student and for general reader.

Hallenbeck, C. Spanish missions of the old Southwest. New York, 1926. (184 p.)

A historical and descriptive account of the Spanish missions in Texas, New Mexico, Arizona, and California.

Hallenbeck, C. and J. H. Williams. Legends of the Spanish Southwest. Glendale, Calif., 1938. (342 p.)

Interesting and entertaining, written for the general reader in the light of recent researches.

Hammond, G. P. and A. Rey (eds.). Obregon's history of 16th century explorations in western America, entitled, Chronicle, commentary, or relation of the ancient and modern discoveries in New Spain and New Mexico. Mexico, 1584. Los Angeles, Calif., 1928. (351 p.)

Two parts: (1) on the conquest of Mexico City, New Galicia, New Vizcaya, and adjacent regions; (2) explorations in New Mexico and neighboring regions by Chamuscado and Espejo towards the end of the 16th century.

Hermann, B. The Louisiana purchase. Washington, D. C.: The Government Printing Office, 1900. (87 p.)

Hildrup, J. S. The missions of California and the old Southwest. Chicago, 1912. (100 p.)

Hodge, F. W. (ed.). Handbook of American Indians north of Mexico. 2 vols., Washington, D. C.: The Government Printing Office, 1907-1910.

An indispensable work on ethnological, geographical, and linguistic data.

Hodge, F. W. and T. H. Lewis (eds.). Spanish explorers in the southern United States, 1528-1543—Original narratives of early American history. New York. 1907. (411 p.)

Contains (1) The narrative of Alvar Nuñez Cabeza de Vaca, ed. by F. W. Hodge (pp. 1-126); (2) The narrative of the expedition of Hernando de Soto, by the Gentleman of Elvas, ed. by T. H. Lewis (pp. 127-272); The narrative of the expedition of Coronado, by Pedro de Castañeda, ed. by F. W. Hodge (pp. 273-387).

Holweck, F. G. "An American martyrology." CHR, VI (1921), 495-516.

Takes the term "martyrology" in its broader sense, to include such missionaries as did not suffer violent death at the hands of the Indians.

Johnson, W. "The early theatre in the Spanish borderlands." M-A, II n.s. (1930). 121-131.

Jones, C. C. Antiquities of the Southern Indians. New York, 1873. (133 p.)

Historical sketch of the Tomo-chi-chi Mico (chief) of the Yama-craws, a refugee band of Creek Indians in Georgia.

Lummis, C. F. Some strange corners of our country: wonderland of the Southwest. New York, 1903. (270 p.)

Macleod, W. C. The American Indian frontier. London and New York, 1928. (598 p.)

Deals with Indians, conquerors, and traders; contrasts Latin and Anglo-Saxon exploits and institutions.

Mecham, J. L. "Francisco de Urdiñola, governor of Nueva Vizcaya." New Spain and the Anglo-American West, Los Angeles, Calif., 1932, I, 39-65.

Mecham, J. L. Francisco de Ibarra and Nueva Vizcaya. Durham: Duke University press, 1927. (265 p.)

Mendizábal, M. O. de. La evolución del noroeste de Mexico. Mexico, D. F., 1930. (139 p.)

Mooney, J. The aboriginal population of America north of Mexico. Washington, D. C.: The Smithsonian Institution, Misc. Coll., LXXX, No. 7, 1928. (40 p.)

Murphy, R. "The journey of Pedro de Rivera, 1724-1728." SHQ, XLI (1937), 125-141.

Newcomb, R. Spanish colonial architecture in the United States. New York, 1937. (130 p.)

New Spain and the Anglo-American West: contributions to Herbert Eugene Bolton. 2 vols., Los Angeles, Calif., priv. print., 1932.

A collection of essays and documents written or edited by students of Professor H. E. Bolton. The first volume deals with colonial Mexico, including the north-frontier borderlands (1535-1821) and the second with the trans-Mississippi West (1805-1849).

Ocaranza, F. Los Franciscanos en las provincias internas de Sonora y Ostimuri. Mexico, D. F., 1933. (277 p.)

Important for the history of the missions in Pimeria Baja and Alta (Upper Sonora and Lower Arizona) after the departure of the Jesuits in 1767.

Ocaranza, F. (ed.). Crónicas y relaciones del occidente de Mexico. 2 vols. Mexico, D. F., 1937, 1939.

Contains original narratives and reports dealing with the advance of Spain into northwestern Mexico and California. A valuable and important collection of primary source materials.

Otero, N. Old Spain in our Southwest. New York, 1936. (192 p.)

Contains interesting stories and legends.

Peixotto, E. Our Hispanic Southwest. New York, 1916. (245 p.)

A descriptive work with numerous pen-drawings by the author who refers to the Spanish mission ruins as "picturesque material that has been sadly neglected by our writers and artists heretofore" (Preface, p. xi).

Priestley, H. I. José de Gálvez, visitor general of New Spain, 1765-1771. Berkeley: University of California press, 1916. (449 p.)

A careful and thorough study, based on primary sources.

Ramírez Cabañas, J. (ed.). Descripción geográfica de los reinos de Nueva Galicia, Nueva Vizcaya y Nuevo León, por D. Alonso de la Mota e Escobár. Mexico, 1940. (238 p.)

A carefully prepared second edition of Mota y Escobár's valuable treatise.

Richardson, R. N. and **C. C. Rister.** The greater Southwest. Glendale, Calif., 1934. (506 p.)

A comprehensive study of developments—economic, social, and cultural—in our Spanish borderlands west of the Mississippi.

Rivera, Pedro de. Diario y derrotero de lo caminado, visto y observado en el discurso de la visita general de precidios, situados en las Provincias Ynternas de Nueva España, qua de orden de su magestad executó D. Pedro de Rivera, brigadier de los reales exercitos. . . . Guatemala, 1736.

Probably a government print; according to Wagner, "the most important printed document extant relating to the frontier provinces" (*The Spanish Southwest*, 363). Pedro de Rivera made the inspection tour between 1724 and 1728, covering 3,982 leagues and penetrating from Mexico City northward into Texas and New Mexico. C. E. Castañeda lists in his bibliography (*Our Catholic Heritage in Texas,* IV, p. 358) a photostat copy of this document which, according to Wagner (*loc. cit.*) comprises thirty-eight folio leaves.

Ryan, E. A. "Diocesan organization in the Spanish colonies." CHR, II (1916), 146-156, 170-186.

Ryan, E. A. "Ecclesiastical jurisdiction in the Spanish colonies." CHR, V (1919), 3-18.

Schurz, W. L. The Manila galleon. New York, 1939. (453 p.)

Scott, F. J. Historical heritage of the lower Rio Grande San Antonio, 1937. (246 p.)

To quote its sub-title: "A historical record of Spanish exploration, subjugation and colonization of the lower Rio Grande valley and the activities of José Escandon, Count of Sierra Gorda, together with the development of towns and ranches under Spanish, Mexican, and Texas sovereignties, 1747-1848."

Shea, J. G. The Catholic Church in colonial days, 1521-1763. New York, 1886. (663 p.)

Volume I of his four-volume work, The Catholic Church in the United States. Books II and V of the first volume deal with the Spanish borderlands. Still useful, though now replaced in numerous instances by researches and studies of more recent date.

Shelby, C. C. (ed.). "Projected French attacks upon the northeastern frontier of New Spain, 1719-1721." HAHR, XIII (1933), 458-472.

Five documents from French archives in Paris, with an introduction by the editor. The documents deal with a projected invasion of New Mexico from Louisiana and the establishment of a French settlement on St. Bernard Bay by Sieur de St. denis.

Smith, W. H. and **R. L. Grismer.** Tales of the Spanish Southwest. New York, 1934. (181 p.)

Covers California, New Mexico, Arizona, and Texas.

Stephen, H. M. and **H. E. Bolton.** (eds.). The Pacific Ocean in history. New York, 1917. (535 p.)

Papers and addresses presented at the Panama-Pacific historical congress, held at San Francisco, Berkeley, and Palo Alto, California, July 19-23, 1915. The following papers deal with the Spanish Borderlands: (1) "The conflict of European nations in the Pacific" by H. M. Stephens: (2) "The share of Spain in the history of the Pacific Ocean" by R. Altamira y Crevea; (3) "The history of California" by J. F. Davis; (4) "The early explorations of Father Garcés on the Pacific slope" by H. E. Bolton; (5) "The reforms of Joseph Galvez in New Spain" by H. I. Priestley; (6) "The founding of San Francisco" by C. E. Chapman; (7) "French intrusion into New Mexico, 1749-1752" by H. E. Bolton; (8) "Speech mixture in New Mexico" by A. M. Espinosa; (9) "St. Vrain's expedition to the Gila in 1826" by T. M. Marshall; "The causes for the failure of Otermin's attempt to reconquer New Mexico, 1681-1682" by C. W. Hackett.

Sullivan, E. C. and A. E. Logie. The story of the old Spanish missions of the Southwest. Chicago and New York, 1927. (217 p.)

Teixidor, F. (ed.). Don Bernardo Gálvez: Noticia y reflexiones sobre la guerra que se tiene con los Apaches en la Provincia de Nueva España. Mexico, 1925.

Tello, A. Libro segundo de la Crónica Miscelanea. Guadalajara, 1891. (913 p.)

The Second Book of the chronicle "wherein is treated the spiritual and temporal conquest of the Holy Province of Xalisco in the new kingdom of Galicia and Nueva Vizcaya and the discovery of New Mexico, by Fray Antonio Tello" (subtitle); edited by José Lopez-Portillo y Rojas, who contributes a bibliographical introduction, noting that the First Book of the chronicle is lost and that the Third Book has little general interest and comparing the present text of the Second Book with the edition published by Joaquín García Icazbalceta in 1866. Tello, a Franciscan of the Province of Jalisco, lived in the seventeenth century and wrote his chronicle in 1650 and 1651. (See No. 47.) Icazb.

Thomas, A. B. Theodoro de Croix and the northern frontier of New Spain, 1776-1783. Norman: University of Oklahoma press, 1941.

Velasco Ceballos, R. (ed.). La administración de D. Frey Antonio María de Bucareli y Ursúa, cuadragésimo sexto virrey de Mexico. 2 vols. Mexico, D. F.: Archivo general de la Nación, 1936.

A valuable collection of documents, a number of which deal with California, with a scholarly introduction on the administration of one of Mexico's greatest viceroys.

Villa-Señor y Sánchez, J. A. Teatro Americano: description general de los reynos, y provincias de la Nueva-España, y sus jurisdicciones. 2 vols. Mexico, 1746-1748.

An official report, in compliance with a royal decree. The second volume has portions dealing with northern Mexico and our Spanish borderlands.

Wagner, H. R. Spanish voyages to the northwest coast of America in the sixteenth century. San Francisco, 1929. (571 p.)

Extremely valuable for a study of the earliest exploring expeditions to the coasts of present California and Oregon, beginning with Francisco de Ulloa and ending with Sabastian de Vizcaino. It appeared previously in vols. VI and VII (1927 and 1928) of the Quarterly of the California Historical Society.

Warner, L. H. "Conveyance of property, the Spanish and Mexican way." NMHR, VI (1931). 334-359.

Whitaker, A. P. The Spanish-American frontier, 1783-1795: the westward movement and the Spanish retreat in the Mississippi valley. Boston, 1927. (255 p.)

A splendid study of Spanish-American diplomacy, showing how diplomatic affairs were influenced by the Mississippi frontier.

White, L. A. Pioneers in American anthropology: the Bandelier-Morgan letters, 1873-1883. Albuquerque: University of New Mexico press, 1940.

Winsor, J. (ed.). Narrative and critical history of America. 8 vols. Boston and New York, 1884-1889.

The Spanish borderlands are dealt with, more or less briefly, in volumes II and VIII. "The narratives of this work are vastly inferior to the critical essays on sources" (J. L. Mecham, HAHR, VII, 1927, p. 243) which were contributed by Justin Winsor and which constitute the real merit and value of the work.

Winsor, J. "Spanish North America." Narrative and Critical History of North America, VIII, 191-270.

An important study of source materials.

Wyllys, R. K. "A short bibliography of works in English on the Spanish missions of the Southwest." ArizHR, IV (1931), 58-61.

Wyllys, R. K. "The Spanish missions of the Southwest." ArizHR, VI (1935), 27-37.

17

II. DISCOVERY AND EXPLORATION, 1513-1561

Aiton, A. S. "The later career of Coronado." AHR, XXX (1925), 299-306.

Aiton, A. S. "Coronado's testimony in the Viceroy Mendozo residencia." NMHR, XXII (1937), 288-330.

Aiton, A. S. "Coronado's first report on the government of New Galicia." HAHR, XIX (1939), 306-313.

Aiton, A. S. (ed.). "Córonado's muster roll." AHR, XLIV (1939), 556-570.

Aiton, A. S. (trans. and ed.). The muster roll and equipment of the expedition of Francisco Vázquez de Coronado. Ann Arbor, Mich., 1939. (28 p.)

"Now translated into English for the first time with an introduction by Arthur S. Aiton for the meeting of the Institute of Latin-American studies, at Ann Arbor on the occasion of the quadricentennial of Coronado's expedition" (subtitle).

Aiton, A. S. (ed.). "Coronado's commission as captain-general." HAHR, XX (1940), 83-87.

Aiton, A. S. Antonio de Mendoza, first viceroy of New Spain. Durham: Duke University press, 1927. (240 p.)

Chapter V of this scholarly work deals with the Coronado and allied expeditions.

Arteaga y S., A. "Fray Marcos de Niza y el descibrimiento de Nuevo Mexico." HAHR, XII (1932), 481-489.

Deals in part with Marcos de Niza's report on his expedition to the Seven Cities of Cíbola.

Baldwin, P. M. "Fray Marcos de Niza and his discovery of the seven cities of Cibola." NMHR, I (1926), 193-223.

The Spanish text and English translation of the friar's report. The study appeared also as a reprint of the Historical Society of New Mexico, Santa Fé, 1926. (55 p.)

Bandelier, A. F. Contributions to the history of the southwestern portion of the United States. Cambridge: Archaeological Institute of America, 1890. (206 p.)

Contains five highly critical studies, four of which deal with early explorations and discoveries by the Spaniards in the trans-Mississippi Southwest between 1530 and 15:39, notably an elaborate study and defense of Fray Marcos de Niza (pp. 106-179).

Bandelier, F. (trans.). The journey of Alvar Nuñez Cabeza de Vaca and his companions from Florida to the Pacific, 1528-1536. New York, 1904. (231 p.)

A translation of Cabeza de Vaca's *Relación* from the rare 1542 imprint by Mrs. Fanny Bandelier with an introduction by her husband, Adolf F. Bandelier. It was published as one of the volumes of the "Trail Makers" series and in *Spanish Explorers in the Southern United States* (1513-1542). (See No. 159.)

Bandelier, A. F. "Fray Juan de Padilla, the first Catholic missionary and martyr in eastern Kansas, 1542." ACQR, XV (1890), 551-565.

In this essay Bandelier traces Coronado's route to Quivira and discusses the location of the region called Quivira.

Bandelier, A. F. "Discovery of New Mexico by Fray Marcos de Niza." NMHR, IV (1929), 28-45.

Baskett, J. N. A study of the route of Coronado. Topeka: Kansas State Historical Society, Collections, XII (1911), No. 6.

Baskett, J. N. "A study of the route of Cabeza de Vaca." SHQ, X (1907), 246-279, 308-340.

Bishop, M. The odyssey of Cabeza de Vaca. New York, 1933. (306 p.)

Bloom, L. B. "The Coronado Bocanegra family alliance." NMHR, XVI (1941), 401-431.

A genealogical study of the families of Francisco Vázquez de Coronado and Hernán Pérez de Bocanegra, the three children of the one marrying the three children of the other.

Bloom, L. B. "Who discovered New Mexico?" NMHR, XV (1940), 101-132.

The author examines the various claimants and decides in favor of Coronado.

Bloom, L. B. "Was Fray Marcos a liar?" NMHR, XVI (1941), 220-225.

Boston, B. "The route of De Soto: Delisle's interpretation." M-A, XI (1929), 277-297.

Boston, B. "The De Soto map." M-A, XXII (1941), 236-250.

Boyd, M. F. "The arrival of De Soto's expedition in Florida." FHQ, XVI (1938), 188-220.

Bourne, E. G. (ed.). Narratives of the career of Hernando de Soto in the conquest of Florida. 2 vols. New York, 1904.

Contains Buckingham Smith's translation of the *True Relation* by the Gentleman of Elvas, his translation of Biedma's *Relation,* and Bourne's own translation of Ranjel's narrative. The two volumes appeared in the "Trail Makers" series. The introduction by the editor is an excellent study of early source materials concerning De Soto and his expedition.

Brannon, P. "The route of De Soto from Cosa to Mauvilla." AP, II (1921), 3-8.

Brannon, P. "Our first white visitor." AP, VII (1922), 21-23.

Deals with the Narváez expedition of 1528 and its entry into what is today Alabama.

Brower, J. V. Memoirs of exploration in the basin of the Mississippi. 8 vols. St. Paul, Minn., 1898-1904.

Two of the volumes under the subtitle "Quivira" and "Harahey" are devoted to the vexing Quivira problem.

Carreño, A. M. "Francisco Vázquez de Coronado." DH, I (1939), 133-144.

Coopwood, B. "The route of Cabeza de Vaca." SHQ, III (1899), 108-140, 177-208, 229-264; IV (1900), 1-32.

Corse, C. D. The fountain of youth. St. Augustine, Fla., priv. print., 1933. (33 p.)

Besides a historical sketch of the city of St. Augustine, the brochure contains a discussion of the search of the fountain of youth by Ponce de Leon in 1513.

Davenport, H. and J. K. Wells. "The first Europeans in Texas, 1528-1536." SHQ, XXII (1919), 11-142, 205-259.

Davenport, H. (ed.). "The expedition of Pánfilo de Narváez by Gonzalo Fernández de Oviedo y Váldez." SHQ, XXVII (1924), 120-139, 217-241, 276-304; XXVIII (1925), 56-74, 122-163.

First English translation of Oviedo's account, published in his *Historia general* in 1547, of the Narváez expedition.

Davis, T. F. "The record of Ponce de León's discovery of Florida, 1513." FHSQ, XI (1932), 5-15.

Davis, T. F. (trans.). "History of Juan Ponce de León's voyages to Florida." FHSQ, XIV (1935), 1-70; also reprint, Jacksonville, Fla., 1935. (70 p.)

Contains translation of contemporary records and accounts.

Day, A. G. Coronado's quest: the discovery of the southwestern states. Los Angeles: University of California press, 1940. (418 p.)

Presents the story of Coronado's exploration and adventures with a study of the historical background.

Day, A. G. "Mota Padilla on the Coronado expedition." HAHR, XX (1940), 88-110.

A translation, with brief introduction, of that portion of Mota Padilla's *Historia*, written in 1742, which treats the Coronado expedition. The introduction is a brief bio-bibliographical account of Mota Padilla.

Donoghue, D. "The route of the Coronado expedition in Texas." SHQ, XXXII (1929), 181-192.

Shows the untenability of earlier theories and presents reasons for locating Quivira on the north bank of the Canadian River in the Texas panhandle.

Donoghue, D. "The route of Coronado in Texas." NMHR, IV (1929), 77-90.

Donoghue, D. "Coronado, Oñate, and Quivira." M-A, XVIII (1936), 85-95; also Preliminary Studies of the Texas Catholic Historical Society, Austin, Texas. (1936), No. 3. (12 p.)

A further attempt by Donoghue to trace the route of Coronado over the Llano Estacado of Texas to the region called Quivira. A chart of Oñate's route is presented as evidence that Quivira lay in the upper regions of the Texas panhandle.

Engelhardt, Z. "Report of Fr. Marcos de Niza." FH, VI (1918), 281-283, 314-318, 353-358, 398-400.

This is an English translation of Marcos de Niza's *Relación* concerning his expedition to the Seven Cities of Cibola in 1539, from the Spanish text in Pacheco y Cardenas, *Colección de documentos inéditos*, III, pp. 325-351.

Engelhardt, Z. "Florida's first bishop: Rt. Rev. Juan Juarez, O.F.M." CHR, IV (1919), 379-385.

Presents evidence that Juan Juarez came to Florida with the Narváez expedition as bishop-elect of the newly discovered region, in 1528.

Foik, P. J. "Fray Juan de Padilla: proto-martyr of the United States and Texas." M-A, XIII (1930), 132-140; also Preliminary Studies of the Texas Catholic Historical Society, Austin, Texas, I (1930), No. 5. (11 p.)

Foik, P. J. "Early Catholic explorers of the Southwest." M-A, XIII (1930), 199-211; also Preliminary Studies of the Texas Catholic Historical Society, Austin, Texas, I (1930), No. 2. (15 p.)

Fordyce, J. R. "De Soto in Arkansas." ArkHR, I (1934). 3-20.

Attempt to trace the route of Soto's army through Arkansas.

Fordyce, J. R. "Explorations of De Soto." ME, XXVIII (1936), 1-6, 114-119.

Garcilaso de la Vega ("The Inca"). La Florída del Ynca. Historia del adelantado, Hernando de Soto, Gouernador, y Capitán General del Reyno de la Florída y de otros heróicos cauelleros, Españoles e Indios. Lisbon, 1605.

One of the earliest sources on the De Soto expedition by an educated Peruvian Indian residing in Spain. A second edition by Barcia appeared in Madrid in 1723. For an estimate of the reliability of *La Florída del Ynca* see Steck's "Neglected aspects of the De Soto expedition" (M-A, XV, n.s., 1932, p. 5, note 5). (See No. 200.)

Gavazzo Perry Vidal, F. (ed.). Relacão verdadeira dos trabalhos que o Governador D. Fernando de Souto e certos fidalgos Portugueses parraram no descobrimento da província da Flórida agora novamente escrita por um fidalgo de Elvas. Lisbon: Agência Geral das Colónias, 1940. (419 p.)

The text and a facsimile reproduction of the De Soto narrative by the Gentleman of Elvas with a bibliographical study by the editor.

Gentleman of Elvas. Relaçam verdadeira dos trabalhos q ho gouernador do Fernãdo d' souto e - certos fidalgos portugueses passaron no d'scobrimēto da prouincia da Frolida. Agora nouamēte feita per hufidalgo Deluas. Foy vista porho señor inquisidor. [Evora: A. de Busgos, 1557] Boston, 1924. facsim., 360 leaves.

This is a photostat reproduction of the original text preserved in the British museum, produced in ten copies by the Massachusetts Historical Society. Photostat Reproductions, American Series, No. 117.

Hallenbeck, C. Alvar Nuñez Cabeza de Vaca. The journey and route of the first European to cross the continent of North America, 1534-1536. Glendale, Calif., 1940. (326 p.)

An elaborate and critical study, divided into three parts: (1) the journey of Alvar Nuñez Cabeza de Vaca, (2) the route of his journey across Texas, (3) his route as traced by others.

Hammond, G. P. and E. F. Goad. The adventures of Francisco Vázquez de Coronado. Albuquerque: University of New Mexico press, 1938. (140 p.)

Hammond, G. P. and A. Rey. Narratives of the Coronado expedition, 1540-1542. Albuquerque: University of New Mexico press, 1940. (413 p.)

This is Vol. II of the Coronado Cuarto-Centennial Publications, 1540-1940. It contains twenty-nine documents on Coronado and his expedition to New Mexico. Without doubt, the finest work on the subject, ranking easily with that of Winship, which is now too difficult to procure.

Hammond, G. P. Coronado's seven cities. Albuquerque, N. M.: U. S. Coronado Exposition Commission, 1940. (82 p.)

Popular in form, but accurate and reliable, by a recognized authority on the subject.

Haro y Cadena, J. (trans.). "La matrícula de revista de la expedicion de Coronado." DH, I (1939), 117-126.

This is a translation of A. S. Aiton's study. See No. 110.

Hernández Díaz, J. Expedición del adelantado Hernando de Soto. Seville, Spain: Instituto Hispano-Cubano de Historia de America, 1938. (47 p.)

A calendar of seventy documents dealing with the organization and equipment of the De Soto expedition to Florida, four documents reproduced in as many appendices. These documents shed new light on the De Soto enterprise.

Hodge, F. W. and T. H. Lewis (eds.). Spanish explorers in the southern United States, 1528-1543—Original narratives of early American history. New York, 1907. (487 p.)

The volume contains: (1) "The narrative of Alvar Nuñez Cabeza de Vaca," edited by F. W. Hodge; (2) "The narrative of the Expedition of Hernando de Soto by the Gentleman of Elvas," edited by T. H. Lewis; (3) "The narrative of the expedition of Coronado, by Pedro de Castañeda," edited by F. W. Hodge. Each of the narratives is preceded by a critical introduction contributed by the editor.

Hodge, F. W. (ed.). "The narrative of the expedition of Coronado, by Pedro de Castañeda," Spanish explorers in the Southern United States—Original narratives of early American history. New York, 1907, pp. 273-387.

Reproduces Winship's translation of the narrative, published in 1896, with an introduction on Castañeda and his work and on source materials dealing with the Coronado expedition.

Hodge, F. W. (ed.). "The narrative of Alvar Nuñez Cabeza de Vaca," Spanish explorers in the Southern United States—Original narratives of early American history. New York, 1907, pp. 1-126.

Reproduces the Buckingham Smith edition, published in 1871, with an introduction on De Vaca and source materials dealing with his adventures.

Irving, T. The conquest of Florida by Hernando de Soto. New York, 1851. (457 p.)

Based on Garcilaso de la Vega's *La Florida del Ynca* and the *Relación* of the Gentleman of Elvas.

Ives, R. L. "Melchior Díaz—the forgotten explorer." HAHR, XVI (1936), 86-90.

A brief study of the expedition which Díaz, in 1540, conducted through Arizona, Sonora, and California.

Ives, R. L. (trans. and ed.). "The report of the bishop of Durango on conditions in Northwestern Mexico in 1745." HAHR, XIX (1939), 314-317.

22

Jones, C. C., Jr. The adventures encountered and the route pursued by [Hernando de Soto] . . . within the present . . . State of Georgia. Savannah, 1880. (43 p.)

Jones, H. "Quivira—Rice County, Kansas." Topeka, Kansas: State Historical Society Collections, XVII (1928), 535-546.

Identifies the site of Quivira and describes Indian relics found there.

Jones, P. A. Quivira. Wichita, Kansas, 1929. (182 p.)

A popular account of the Coronado expedition in which the author defends the theory that Quivira was located in Kansas.

Jones, P. A. Coronado and Quivira. Lyons, Kansas, 1937. (242 p.)

This is the third and revised edition of the author's *Quivira*, published in 1929. The first part reprints the earlier work, omitting the chapter on "The tradition of Modoc" and adding a new chapter on "The lure of gold." The second part, twelve chapters, contains the author's study and conclusion regarding the route followed by Coronado, reprints A. S. Aiton's article on "The last days of Coronado," and reproduces La Barra's study of Coronado's genealogy.

Johnson, J. G. "A Spanish settlement in Carolina, 1526." GHQ, VII (1923), 339-345.

Tells the story of the Vázquez de Ayllon's short-lived colony on the Atlantic coast.

León de la Barra, L. and García Abello. "Apuntes genealogicos sobre Francisco Vázquez de Coronado." DH, I (1939), 533-538.

Lewis, T. H. "Route of De Soto's expedition from Taliepacana to Huhasene." Jackson: Publications of the Mississippi Historical Society, VI (1902), 449-467.

Lewis, T. H. "De Soto's route." AP, XX (1935), 16-18.

Reproduction of a letter of Theodore H. Lewis, dated June 14, 1894, in which the writer furnishes data to identify localities in the Gulf region visited by the De Soto expedition and mentioned in the narrative of the Gentleman of Elvas and of others.

Lewis, T. H. (ed.). "The narrative of the expedition of Hernando de Soto by the Gentleman of Elvas." Spanish Explorers in the southern United States—Original narratives of early American history, New York, 1907, pp. 127-272.

Reproduces Buckingham Smith's translation, published in 1866, with an introduction on the Gentleman of Elvas, the character of his narrative, and earlier editions and translations of the narrative.

López-Portillo y Weber, J. "Las provincias de Avalos." DH, III (1941), 164-167.

Contains some biographical data on Fray Juan de Padilla before his coming to New Mexico with the Coronado expedition.

López-Portillo y Weber, J. La rebellión de Nueva Galicia. Tacubaya, Mexico, 1939. (594 p.)

Contains a study of the Mixton war of 1541 in Northwestern Mexico between Spaniards and Indians at a time when Coronado's expedition was under way.

Love, W. A. "Route of De Soto's expedition through Lowndas County, Mississippi." AP, VIII (1923), 85-92; also Jackson: Publications of the Mississippi Historical Society, Centenary Series, IV (1921), 268-276.

Lowery, W. The Spanish settlements within the present limits of the United States, 1513-1561. 1st edition, 1901; 2nd edition, 1911. (515 p.)

Deals with the early Spanish discoveries and explorations in our southern borderlands, east and west of the Mississippi, 1513-1561. A pioneer work in the field, scholarly and exhaustive, and still a standard work, though in some matters superseded by more recent researches and studies.

Maynard, T. De Soto and the conquistadores. New York, 1930. (297 p.)

A literary rather than a scientific work. Chapters VIII to XIX (pp. 116-278) deal with De Soto after his return from Peru and with his Florida enterprise.

Oblasser, B. His own personal narrative, or Arizona discovered by Fray Marcos de Niza . . . Topawa, Arizona, 1939. (32 p.)

Based on personal journeyings in Mexico and Arizona, this is a most careful translation of the friar's account "from the original in the Archives of the Indies, Seville, Spain," with six charts by the author and a Foreword by Frank C. Lockwood. The author defends the veracity of Fray Marcos de Niza.

O'Daniel, V. F. Dominicans in early Florida. New York, 1930. (230 p.)

Biographical sketches of twenty-four Dominicans who were active in Florida during the sixteenth century (1526-1561), ending with Bishop Las Cabezas y Altamirano of Santiago de Cuba, who held the first canonical visitation in Florida (1606).

Perea, J. A. and **S.** Historia del adelantado Juan Ponce de León. Caracas, 1929. (119 p.)

Pérez Cabrera, J. M. El capitan Hernando de Soto, Havana; Academía de la Historia de Cuba, 1939. (28 p.)

Contains some new matter concerning the De Soto expedition.

Phinney, A. H. "Narváez and De Soto—their landing places and the town of Espíritu Santo." FHSQ, II (1925), 15-21.

Ponton, B. and **B. H. McFarland.** "Alvar Nuñez Cabeza de Vaca: a preliminary report on his wanderings in Texas." SHQ, I (1897), 166-186.

Priestley, H. I. Tristán de Luna, conquistador of the old South: a study of Spanish imperial strategy. Glendale, Calif., 1936. (215 p.)

Priestley, H. I. (trans. and ed.). The Luna papers: documents relating to the expedition of Don Tristán de Luna y Arellano for the conquest of La Florida in 1559-1561. 2 vols. Deland: Florida State Historical Society Publications, No. 8, 1928.

Indispensable documents pertaining to the De Luna expedition, with a scholarly introduction by the editor and translator. The documents are for the most part from the Archivo General de las Indias in Seville, Spain.

Reynolds, C. B. The landing of Ponce de León, a historical review. Mountain Lakes, N. J., priv. publ., 1934. (31 p.)

A criticism of "The fountain of youth" by C. D. Corse. (See No. 134.)

Richelet, P. Histoire de la conquête de la Floride ou relation de ce qui s'est passé dans la decouverte de ce pays par Ferdinand de Soto. Laide, 1731.

This is a French translation of Garcilaso de la Vega's La Florida del Ynca.

Robertson, J. A. (ed.). "Letter of De Soto to the secular cabildo of Santiago de Cuba." FHSQ, XVI (1938), 174-178.

Robertson, J. A. (trans. and ed.). True relation of the hardships suffered by Governor Fernando de Soto and certain Portuguese gentlemen during the discovery of the province of Florida. Now set forth by a gentleman of Elvas. 2 vols. Deland: The Florida Historical Society, 1932 and 1933.

An elaborate and critical translation of the Elvas narrative of the De Soto expedition, based on the original Portuguese "facsimile reproduction . . . made from the copy of the original 'Relacam' of 1557 owned by the New York Public Library" (Foreword).

Sauer, C. O. "The discovery of New Mexico reconsidered." NMHR, XII (1937), 270-287.

The author seeks to overthrow the claim of Marcos de Niza as to his expedition into New Mexico.

Sauer, C. O. "The credibility of the Fray Marcos Account." NMHR, XVI (1941), 233-243.

Reply to Bloom's "Who discovered New Mexico?" (NMHR, XV, 1940, pp. 101-132). Answers two questions: (1) Does Fray Marcos's account in general show good faith? (2) Is Fray Marcos's calendar reasonable or possible? He compares a photostat copy of the friar's report with the Pacheco-Cárdenas version.

Sauer, C. O. The road to Cibola. Berkeley: University of California press, Ibero-Americana, III, 1932. (58 p.)

The author discusses explorations made by the Spaniards into Northwestern Mexico and our Southwest. He discredits the report of Marcos de Niza.

Shine, M. "The lost province of Quivira." CHR, II (1916), 3-18.

Smith, T. Buckingham. Colección de varios documentos para la historia de la Florida y tierras adyacentes. Madrid, 1857. (208 p.)

Only the first of this contemplated monumental work appeared. The documents, mostly from the Simancas archives, number thirty-three papers from 1516 to 1569 and five from 1618 to 1794.

Solar y Tabaoda, A. and **J. de Rujula y de Ochotorena.** El adelantado Hernando de Soto: breves noticias, nuevos documentos para su biografía y relación de los que la acompañaron a la Florida. Badajos, 1929. (334 p.)

Swanton, J. R. "The landing place of De Soto." FHQ, XVI (1938), 149-173.

Swanton, J. R. Final report of the United States De Soto expedition. Commission, 76th Congress, 1st session, House Document, No. 71. Washington, D. C.: Government Printing Office, 1939. (400 p.)

The report, drawn up by J. R. Sawnton as chairman of the Commission, is important for fixing the route followed by the De Soto expedition.

Steck, F. B. The Jolliet-Marquette expedition, 1673. Washington, D. C.: The Catholic University of America press, 1927; 2nd edition, Glendale, California, 1928. (334 p.)

The Introduction (pp. 1-48) deals with "the problem of the northern mystery and the discovery of the Mississippi" by the Spaniards in the sixteenth century.

Steck, F. B. "Neglected aspects of the De Soto expedition." M-A. XV (1932), 3-26.

Stoner, V. R. "The discovery of Arizona." Ka, IV (1939), 27-30.

Strickland, R. W. "Moscoso's journey through Texas." SHQ, XLVI (1942), 109-137.

Deals with the attempt of the De Soto army to return, after their leader's death, over Texas to Mexico under the command of Luis de Moscoso.

Vedia, D. Enrique de (ed.). Historiadores primitivos—Biblioteca de autores españoles, vols. 22 and 26. Madrid, 1918, 1923.

The first volume contains López de Gomara's *Historia general de las Indias* and *Conquista de Mexico* (pp. 155-455). In the *Historia* are accounts of Ponce de Leon's discovery of Florida (180-181), the expedition of Pánfilo de Narváez (181-183), the enterprise of Francisco de Garay (183), the penetration into northwestern Mexico by Guzmán and into New Mexico by Marcos de Niza and Coronado (286-289); while the *Conquista* has accounts of Pineda's voyage along the gulf coast (324-325), Cortés's dealings with Narváez in Mexico (359-362), the 1523 voyage of Francisco de Garay along the gulf coast to the Rio de las Palmas and the Pánuco (397-398). As chaplain of Cortés, Gómara had access to documents which make these accounts worth noting.

Wagner, H. R. "Fr. Marcos de Niza." NMHR, IX (1934), 184-227; also 336-337.

A critical examination of Niza's much-discussed report concerning the Seven Cities of Cibola, New Mexico; also an excerpt from a letter of Coronado to the emperor, dated Compostela, July 15, 1539, which concerns Fray Marcos de Niza.

Wagner, H. R. The Spanish Southwest. Albuquerque: University of New Mexico press, 1937. (553 p.)

This is Vol. VII (in two parts) of the Quivira Society *Publications*, a magnificent bibliography. It contains a thorough bio-bibliographical study of Cabeza de Vaca (pp. 29-50). There are similar, though briefer, studies of Marcos de Niza (pp. 89-103), Francisco de Ulloa (pp. 105-115), Fernando Alarcón (pp. 115-116).

Williams, J. W. "Moscoso's trail in Texas." SHQ, XLVI (1942), 138-158.

Deals with the attempt of the Spaniards under Luís de Moscoso, after De Soto's death, to return to Mexico by an overland route.

Williams, J. W. "Route of Cabeza de Vaca in Texas." SHQ, III (1899), 54-64.

Wilson, S. L. "The relation of the Ohio River and its valleys to the discovery of the Mississippi by De Soto." FCHQ, XVI (1942), 55-66.

Winship, G. P. (ed. and trans.). The Coronado Expedition, 1540-1542. Fourteenth Annual Report of the Bureau of Ethnology. Washington, D. C.: Government Printing Office, 1896. Part I, pp. 329-637.

A pioneer work, scientific and exhaustive, the result of many years of research and study and of wide correspondence with the outstanding scholars of the day in this country and abroad. Will always remain the standard work on the Coronado enterprise together with the *Narratives of the Coronado Expedition* by G. P. Hammond and A. Rey, who can concede that "Without the guidance provided by the pioneer labors of Winship and Hodge, our task would have been more difficult and the results of our study less perfect" (p. 32).

Woldert, A. "The expedition of Luís de Moscoso in Texas in 1542." SHQ, XLVI (1942), 158-166.

The remnants of the De Soto expedition in Texas, after De Soto's death, on their attempted return journey to Mexico.

26

III. FLORIDA, 1561-1819

Abbey, K. T. Florida, Land of Change. Chapel Hill: University of North Carolina press, 1941. (426 p.)

Rather popular than strictly scientific, emphasizing the period since 1819.

Abbey, K. T. "Spanish projects for the reoccupation of the Floridas during the American revolution," HAHR, IX (1929), 265-285.

Anderson, J. R. "The Spanish era in Georgia, and the English settlement in 1733." GHQ, XVII (1933), 91-108.

Deals with the Spanish regime in Georgia during the 16th and 17th centuries.

Arthur, S. C. The story of the West Florida rebellion. St. Francisville, La., 1935. (164 p.)

Averrette, A. (ed. and trans.) The unwritten history of old St. Augustine. St. Augustine, Fla., 1902.

The documentary portion of this volume "must be used with great care because of many inaccuracies, including numerous instances of misdating" (Chatelain, *The Defenses of Spanish Florida,* 1565 to 1763, p. 98).

Barcía Carballido y Zuñiga, A. G. Ensayo cronológico para la historia general de la Florida, 1512-1722. Madrid, 1723. (366 p.)

Though here and there inaccurate, still valuable, being based on sources no longer available. Published under the pseudonym Gabriel de Cardenas Z. Cano.

Barreiro, A. "Descripción de la Florida oriental hecha en 1787. Por el teniente de navio, D. José del Río Cossa." Mexico, D. F.: Archivo General de la Nación, Boletín, LXXV (1935), 420-432, 456-460.

First publication of the document with annotations by A. Barreiro.

Barrientos, B. Vida y hechos de Pero Menéndez de Auilés, Cauellero de la horden de Sanctiago, adelantado de la Florida [1568].

A contemporary biography of the founder of Spanish Florida, published for the first time by Genaro García in *Dos Antiguas* Relaciones de Florida (Mexico, 1902), pp. 1-154. It is based, apparently, on sources no longer extant.

Basanier (ed.). L'Histoire notable de la Floride située en Indes Occidentales, contenant les trois voyages faits en icelle par certains capitaines et pilotes francois, descrits par le capitaine Laudoniere, qui y a cammandé l'espace d'un an trois moys. Paris, 1586.

Laudonniere's *Histoire,* as edited by Basanier in 1586, contains four parts, the first three being the narratives of Laudoniere and the fourth the narrative of Gourges. Hakluyt published an English version in 1853 and this version B. F. French embodied in his *Historical Collections of Louisiana and Florida* (New York, 1869), pp. 165-346. Gaffarel, in his *Histoire de la Floride Française* (Paris, 1875) prints in full (pp. 347-376) the first part and selected extracts (pp. 377-401) of the second and third parts of Laudonniere's Histoire, while the last portion of the volume (pp. 483-515) brings the report of Gourges entitled "La Reprinse de la Floride."

Bayle, C. "Justificaciones históricas: Pedro Menéndez de Avilés." RyF, LXIX (1924), 409-424.

A defense of Menéndez de Avilés in connection with action against the Huguenots under Ribaut in 1565.

Bayle, C. Pedro Menéndez de Avilés. Madrid, 1928. (153 p.)

Biggar, H. M. and **J. T. Connor.** The whole and true discouerye of Terra Florida; a facsimile reprint of the London edition of 1563, together with a transcript of an English version in the British Museum with notes by H. M. Biggar, and a biography by Jeannette Thurber Connor. De Land: The Florida Historical Society, 1927. (139 p.)

27

Bleron, E. "The St. Augustine historical restoration." FHQ, XVI (1937), 110-118.

Bocock, N. F. "William Stephens." GHQ, XVII (1933), 243-248.

Stephens was connected in an official capacity with the founding and early history of English Georgia.

Bohnenberger, C. "The settlement of Charlotia (Robles Town), 1765." FHQ, IV (1925), 43-49.

Discusses an early attempt by the English to found a colony in Florida.

Bolton, H. E. (ed.). Arredondo's historical proof of Spain's title to Georgia. Berkeley: University of California press, 1925. (382 p.)

Prints the English translation and the original Spanish text. Deals with the Spanish-English conflict over the coastlands of Georgia and South Carolina. The introduction (pp. 1-110), entitled *The Debatable Land,* is a scholarly study and was published separately.

Bolton, H. E. and **M. Ross.** The debatable land, a sketch of the Anglo-Spanish contest for the Georgia country. Berkeley: University of California press, 1925. (138 p.)

Based for the most part on manuscript sources with invaluable information concerning these manuscripts and pertinent secondary sources.

Bolton, H. E. "Spanish resistance to the Carolina traders in western Georgia." GHQ, IX (1925), 115-130.

Boyd, M. F. "The fortifications at San Marcos de Apalache." FHSQ, XV (1936), 3-34.

Boyd, M. F. "Expedition of Marcos Delgado, 1686." FHSQ, XVI (1937), 2-32.

Boyd, M. F. "Spanish mission sites in Florida." FHSQ, XVII (1939), 254-280.

Boyd, M. F. "From a remote frontier." FHSQ, XXI (1942), 44-52.

"Letters and reports passing between the commanders at Apalache (St. Mark's), Governor Grant at St. Augustine, General Haldiman at Pensacola, and General Gage, commander-in-chief at New York, 1767-1679" (subtitle).

Brinton, D. G. Notes on the Florida peninsula, its literary history, Indian tribes, and antiquities. Philadelphia, 1859. (202 p.)

Brooks, P. C. Diplomacy and the borderlands. The Adams-Onís Treaty of 1819. Berkeley: University of California Publications in History, XXIV, 1939.

Brown, P. W. "Salamanca and the beginnings of the Church in Florida." ER, LXXXIV (1931), 581-587.

Deals with the services of priests from the University of Salamanca in Florida, the first two arriving at St. Augustine in 1784.

Burrage, H. S. (ed.). Early English and French voyages, chiefly from Hakluyt, 1534-1608 — Original Narratives of Early American History. New York, 1906. (419 p.)

Contains (pp. 111-132) John Sparke's description of Hawkins's voyage to the Florida coast in 1565.

Candler, A. D. (ed.). The colonial records of the State of Georgia. Atlanta, 1906-1907.

Carroll, B. R. (ed.). Historical collections of South Carolina, embracing many rare and valuable pamphlets and other documents, relating to the history of that state, from its first discovery to its independence in the year 1776. 2 vols. New York, 1936.

Cate, M. Our todays and yesterdays. A story of Brunswick and the coastal islands. Brunswick, Ga., 1926; rev. ed., 1930. (302 p.)

Caughey, J. W. (trans). McGillivray of the Creeks. Norman: University of Oklahoma press. 1938. (385 p.)

Contains 214 documents translated from the Spanish and covering the years 1783-1794, with a critical life sketch of McGillivray.

Caughey, J. W. "Alexander McGillivray and the Creek crisis, 1783-1784." New Spain and the Anglo-American West. Los Angeles, 1932. I, 263-288.

Chapin, G. M. Florida, 1513-1913, past, present, and future; four hundred years of wars and peace and industrial development. 2 vols. Chicago, 1914.

Chatelain, V. E. The defenses of Spanish Florida, 1565 to 1763. Washington, D. C.: Carnegie Institution of Washington, publ. 511, 1941. (192 p.)

Scholarly, and heavily documented, with four attractive illustrations and twenty-two charts of inestimable value for the history of Spanish Florida.

Cole, E. K. "Charles Fort, South Carolina, built by Ribault in 1562." Huguenot Society of South Carolina, Transactions, XXIX (1925), 15-25.

Seeks to identify the site of the fort erected by Jean Ribault on the present Parris Island.

Connor, J. T. and H. M. Biggar (ed.). Jean Ribault. The whole and true discouerye of Terra Florida. (See No. 220.)

Connor, J. T. (ed. and trans.). Colonial records of Spanish Florida. Deland: Florida State Historical Society, Publications. 2 vols. 1925 and 1930.

A masterly work, indispensable for the history of Florida from 1570 to 1580. Spanish text and English translation.

Connor, J. T. (ed. and trans.). Pedro Menéndez de Avilés, adelantado, governor and captain-general of Florida Memorial by Gonzalo Solís de Merás. First published in La Florida, su conquista y colonización por Pedro

Menéndez de Avilés by Eugenio Ruidíaz y Caravia. Deland: Florida State Historical Society, Publications, 1923. (286 p.)

The best English translation of the Merás narrative, "the principal contemporary account of the life and times of Pedro Menéndez de Avilés."

Connor, J. T. "The nine old wooden forts of St. Augustine." FHSQ, IV (1926), 103-111, 171-180.

Corbitt, D. C. "The contention over the superintendencia of the Floridas [1812-1816]." FHSQ, XV (1936), 113-117.

Discusses the rival claims of the captain-general of Louisiana and the intendant of Cuba.

Corbitt, D. C. "James Colbert and the Spanish claims to the east bank of the Mississippi." MVHR, XXIV (1938), 457-472.

Discusses the seizures of boats by Colbert along the Mississippi River.

Corbitt, D. C. (trans. and ed.). "Papers relating to the Georgia-Florida frontier, 1784-1800." GHQ, XXIII (1939), 77-79, 189-202, 300-304, 381-387.

Translations of the William Panton correspondence.

Corbitt, D. C. "The return of Spanish rule to the St. Mary's and the St. John's, 1813-1821." FHQ, XX (1941), 60-74.

Corry, J. P. Indian affairs in Georgia, 1732-1756. Philadelphia: University of Pennsylvania press, 1935. (197 p.)

Seeks to clarify the part played by the Indians in the struggle between Spain, France, and England for control in the west and southwest of Georgia.

Corse, C. D. The key to the golden islands. Chapel Hill: University of North Carolina press, 1931. (165 p.)

The history of Ft. George Island, in Florida, from 1562 to 1926.

Corse, C. D. "Denys Rolle and Rollestown, a pioneer for Utopia." FHSQ, VII (1928), 115-134.
Deals with the attempt of Denys Rolle to found a colony in Florida, based on English primary sources.

Coulter, E. M. (ed.). Georgia's disputed ruins. Chapel Hill: University of North Carolina press, 1937. (275 p.)
Seeks to prove that the ancient structures are not Spanish mission ruins but English sugar mills.

Cox, I. J. The West Florida controversy, 1798-1813. Baltimore, 1918. (699 p.)

Cox, I. J. "Florida avanzada fronteriza de Nueva España." SegCIHA (Buenos Aires, 1938), II, 173-184.

Coxe, D. A. A description of the English province of Carolina, by the Spaniards called Florida, and by the French La Louisiane. London, 1727. (122 p.)

Crane, V. W. The southern frontier, 1670-1732. Durham: Duke University press, 1928. (391 p.)
Based for the most part on English sources.

Crane, V. W. "The Tennessee River as the road to Carolina: the beginnings of exploration and trade." MVHR, III (1916), 3-18.

Crane, V. W. "The origin of the name of the Creek Indians." MVHR, V (1918), 339-342.

Cubberly, F. "John Quincy Adams and Florida." FHSQ, V (1926), 88-93.

Cubberly, F. "Fort George (St. Michael), Pensacola." FHSQ, VI (1928), 220-234.

Curley, M. J. Church and state in the Spanish Floridas (1783-1822). Washington, D. C.: The Catholic University of America press, 1940. (380 p.)

Curry, K. "Jean Ribaut, his personality and achievements." FHSQ, VII (1929), 159-163.

Dau, F. W. Florida, old and new. New York, 1934. (377 p.)
A popular account, covering the entire history of Florida.

Davis, T. F. "Macgregor's invasion of Florida, 1817; together with an account of his successors, Irwin, Hubbard and Aury on Amelia Island, East Florida." FHSQ, VII (1928), 3-31; also reprint, Deland: The Florida Historical Society Publications. (73 p.)

Davis, T. F. "United States troops in Spanish East Florida, 1812-13." FHSQ, IX (1930), 3-23, 96-116, 135-155, 259-278.
Prints letter by Lieut. Col. Thomas Adam Smith, who commanded the United States regulars in Florida in 1812-1813.

De Brahm, W. G. "History of the three provinces, South Carolina, Georgia and East Florida." [1771.] Manuscript history in Harvard College Library, Cambridge.
"De Brahm, who was surveyor general of East Florida during the earlier part of the English period, has, in his 'History,' carefully stated the lines of development followed by the Spaniards in Florida during their first period of occupation, as evidenced from the conditions found by the English in 1764, when they assumed control of this region" (Chatelain: *The Defenses of Spanish Florida 1565 to 1763*, p. 98).

Dewhurst, W. W. The history of St. Augustine, Florida. N. Y., 1886. (182 p.)

DeRenne, W. J. (trans.). [Official Spanish account of the attack on Georgia.] Savannah: Georgia Historical Society, Collections, VII, pt. 2, 1913.
Original documents from the Archivo General de las Indias, Seville, Spain.

Dewhurst, W. W. "Disputes between the United States and Spain over Florida settled by the treaty of 1819." Orlando: 15th an. sess. Florida State Bar Association, 1922, 103-118.
A discussion from a legal point of view of rival land and other claims in West Florida.

Dickinson, J. Narrative of a shipwreck in the Gulf of Florida.
Philadelphia, 1697; 4th ed.,
1751.

A narrative and descriptive journal, whose lengthy original title
read: "God's Protecting Providence,
Man's Surest Help and Defense in
Time of the greatest Difficulty, and
most Eminent Danger Evidenced in
the remarkable Deliverance of Rob-
ert Barrow, with divers other Persons, from the devouring waves of
the Sea; among which they suffered
Shipwreck; and also from the cruel,
devouring Jaws of the inhuman
Canibels of Florida, Faithfully related by Jonathan Dickinson, one of
the Persons concerned therein."
(See Chatelain, *The Defenses of
Spanish Florida 1565 to 1763.* p.
100.)

Document. "James Monroe, Secretary of State, to George Matthews." FHSQ, VI (1928), 235-
237.

The letter, dated April 4, 1812,
disapproves the measures taken by
Matthews to obtain Amelia Island
and other lands from the Spaniards.

Document. "Address of the 'principal inhabitants of East Flori a'
to Governor Tonyn, June 6,
1783." FHSQ, VIII (19:),
169-173.

Contains a list of the "Princ i
inhabitants of East Florida" at t..e
time of the cession.

Document. "Letters of John Innerarity." FHSQ, IX (1931), 67-
89, 127-134; X (1932), 134-138,
185-194; XI (1933), 33-39, 88-
90, 140-141; XII (1934), 37-41,
84-88.

John Innerarity was a partner in
the John Forbes and Co., successors
to the Panton, Leslie and Co.

Document. "The Panton, Leslie
papers." FHSQ, VIII (1930),
131-142.

The first installment of original
documents—the records of Panton,
Leslie and Co. and of their successors, John Forbes and Co. The
records appear hereafter continuously in the issues of the *Florida
Historical Society Quarterly.*

Document. "The Creek Nation,
debtor to John Forbes and co.,
successors to Panton, Leslie and
co.; a journal of John Innerarity,
1812." FHSQ, IX (1930), 67-
89.

Document. "Statutes relating to
Florida, in the diocesan synod,
held by his majesty's command,
by the Rt. 'Rev. Dr. John García
de Palacios, Bishop of Cuba, in
June, 1684." USCHM (1887),
287-297.

Document. "A talk to the Creek
nation . . . [and] a letter from
Daniel McGillivray to William
Panton, respecting William Au-
gustus Bowles." FHSQ, XI
(1932), 33-39.

Document. Letter of Bishop Toral
to Pedro Menéndez de Avilés,
Merida, Yucatan, April 5, 1567.
Cartas de Indias (Madrid: Min-
isterio de Fomento, 1877), 238-
241.

Announces receipt of letter from
Menendez and impending shipment
of supplies and offers advice on how
to govern well in Florida.

Document. "Apalachee during the
British occupation; a description
contained in a series of four reports by Lieut. Pittman, R.E."
FHSQ, XII (1934), 114-122.

Document. "The Panton, Leslie
papers." FHSQ, VIII (1930)
131-142; and following to vol.
XV (1937), 124-134.

Document. "Dispatches of Spanish
officials bearing on the free
Negro settlement of Gracia Real
de Santa Teresa de Mose,
Florida [1688-1759]." JNH, IX
(1924), 144-195.

Document. Reglamento para las
peculiares obligaciones de el
presidio de San Augustin de la
Florida, y reglas que en élse
deben observar, mediante a lo
dispuesto, para la tropa, que le
ha de guarnecer. En el reglamento formado para la Habana.
Año de 1753. Hecho por el
excmo. señor conde de Revilla
Gigedo . . . Mexico [1753].
Boston: Massachusetts Historical
Society, Photostat Americana,
2nd ser., No. 20, 1936.

Fifteen copies were made of this
reglamento from the original preserved in the John Carter Brown
library.

Document. Derrotero de la expedición en la provincia de los Texas, nuevo reyno de Philipinas, que de orden del excmo. señor marqués de Velero, vi-rey, y capitan general de esta Nueva-España passa a executar el muy illustre señor d. Joseph de Azlor, cavallero mesnadero del reyno de Aragon, marques de S. Miguel de Aguayo . . . que escribe el br. d. Juan Antonio de la Peña. Mexico, año de 1722. Boston: Massachusetts Historical Society, Photostat Americana, 2nd ser., No. 17, 1936.

Dunlop, J. G. "Letter from Edmund White to Joseph Morton. Notes by M. B. Webber." SCHM, XXX (1929), 1-5.

The letter is dated in London, February 29, 1687.

Dunlop, J. G. "Spanish depredations, 1686." SCHM, XXX (1929), 81-89.

Relates the destruction of Stuart Town by the invading Spaniards.

Dunlop, J. G. "Captain Dunlop's voyage to the southward, 1687." SCHM, XXX (1929), 127-133.

Journal of Dunlop's expedition to Southern Georgia and Northern Florida.

Dunn, W. E. "The occupation of Pensacola Bay, 1689-1698." FHSQ, IV (1925), 3-14, 76-89; V (1926), 140-154.

Dunn, W. E. "Pirates and miracles in Saint Augustine." CW, CXXVII (1938), 596-600.

Tells of Englishmen from Carolina penetrating into Florida where they were arrested by the Spaniards, taken to St. Augustine, brought before the governor, and charged with piracy.

Dunn, W. E. Spanish and French rivalry in the Gulf region of the United States, 1678-1702. Austin: University of Texas, 1917. (238 p.)

An important study, based on original sources.

Engelhardt, Z. "Missionary labors of the Franciscans among the Indians of the early days (Florida)." FH, I (1913), 110-112, and volumes following.

The articles ran uninterruptedly in the *Franciscan Herald* through Vols. I and II. In the light of what were then (1913) the best Spanish sources, the story is told from the first entry of the Franciscans into Florida down to the end of the colonial period of Florida history.

Engelhardt, Z. "Florida's first bishop, Rt. Rev. Juan Juarez." CHR, IV (1919), 479-485.

Ettinger, A. A. James Edward Oglethorpe, imperial idealist. Oxford: Clarendon press, 1936. (348 p.)

A critical biography based on Spanish as well as English original sources.

Fairbanks, G. R. History and Antiquities of St. Augustine, Florida, with some of the interesting portions of the early history of Florida. New York, 1858. (117 p.)

What is "apparently a second and enlarged edition" (Chatelain, *The Defenses of Spanish Florida, 1565 to 1763*, p. 102) of this work appeared in Jacksonville in 1868 under the title *The Spaniards in Florida, Comprising the Notable Settlement of the Huguenots in 1564 and the History and Antiquities of St. Augustine, Founded A. D. 1565.*

Fairbanks, G. R. History of Florida from its discovery by Ponce de Leon, in 1512, to the close of the Florida War, in 1842. Philadelphia and Jacksonville, 1871. (350 p.)

Fairbanks begins the history of Florida with the mutual signing of the capitulation between king and explorer (1512) and not with the actual landing of Ponce de León in Florida (1513).

Faye, S. "Spanish fortifications of Pensacola, 1698-1763." FHQ, XX (1941), 151-168.

Forbes, J. G. Sketches, historical and topographical, of the Floridas, more particularly of East Florida. New York, 1821. (226 p.)

Forbes, G. "The international conflict for the lands of the Creek confederacy." CO, XIV (1936), 478-498.

Ford, L. C. The triangular struggle for Spanish Pensacola, 1689-1739. Washington, D. C. The Catholic University of America press, 1939. (175 p.)

Gaffarel, P. Histoire de la Floride Francaise. Paris, 1875. (522 p.)

Part Two of the volume contains the accounts by Laudonnière, Le Challeux, and Gourges, the letters and state papers of Forquevaulx, and several smaller accounts pertaining to French activities in Florida in the middle 16th century.

Gallardo, J. M. "The Spaniards and the English settlement in Charles Town." SCHGM, XXXVII (1936), 49-64, 91-99, 131-141.

Translation of Spanish documents (1672-1674) "dealing with the English settlement in Charles Town . . . revealing the attitude of the Spaniards towards the settlement" and containing "information on Charles Town obtained from eye-witnesses."

García, Genaro (ed.). Dos antiguas relaciones de la Florida. Mexico, 1902. (226 p.)

Contains two documents, published here for the first time, viz., (1) Vida y hechos de Pedro Menéndez de Avilés and (2) Relacion de los trabajos que la gente de una nao padeció, por Fray Andrés de San Miguel.

Gatchet, A. S. A migration legend of the Creek Indians. Philadelphia, 1884.

Geiger, M. "The early Franciscans in Florida and their relation to Spain's colonial effort." A. Curtis Wilgus (ed.). Colonial Hispanic America (Washington, D. C.: George Washington University press, 1936), 539-550.

Geiger, M. The Franciscan conquest of Florida, 1573-1618. Washington, D. C.: The Catholic University of America press, 1937. (319 p.)

The author "has made good use of photostats and transcripts of Spanish records available in the United States, especially the photostats in the Stetson Collection; and

although himself a Franciscan, he has presented the evidence in an impartial and scholarly fashion." (Chatelain, *The Defenses of Spanish Florida, 1565 to 1763*. p. 102.)

Geiger, M. (trans.). The martyrs of Florida (1513-1616), by Luís Gerónimo de Oré, O.F.M. New York, 1936. (145 p.)

Translation, with biographical introduction and notes, of Gerónimo de Orés *Relación de los mártires que ha habido en las Provincias de* la Florida.

Geiger, M. Biographical dictionary of the Franciscans in Spanish Florida and Cuba (1528-1841). Paterson, N. J.: St. Anthony Guild press, 1940. (140 p.)

A valuable reference work.

Glodt, J. T. "Our Florida martyr priests" ER, XLI (1923), 498-513, 614-631.

Treats the martyrdom of missionary friars in Spanish Florida between 1549 and 1704.

Greenslade, M. T. "William Panton." FHSQ, XIV (1935), 107-129.

A biography based in part on hitherto unpublished letters which throw light on the character of Panton.

Greenslade, M. T. "John Innerarity, 1783-1854." FHSQ, IX (1930), 90-95.

Griffin, C. C. The United States and the disruption of the Spanish empire. 1810-1822: A study of the relations of the United States with Spain and with the rebel Spanish colonies. New York: Columbia University press, 1937. (315 p.)

Hanna, A. J. "Union catalogue of Floridiana." 'HAHR, XXII (1942), 775-776.

A scientific project that deserves support and co-operation.

Hawkins, B. A sketch of the Creek country in 1798 and 1799. New York, 1848. (88 p.)

Hewatt, A. Historical account of the rise and progress of the colonies of South Carolina and Georgia. 2 vols. London, 1st ed., 1779.

Howard, C. N. "The interval military government in West Florida." LHQ, XXII (1939), 18-30.

Conditions at the transfer of the territory to England in 1763.

Howard, C. N. "Colonial Pensacola: the British period. Part I." FHSQ, XIX (1940), 109-127.

Johnson, J. G. "The Yamassee revolt of 1597 and the destruction of the Georgia missions." GHQ, VII (1923), 44-53.

Johnson, J. G. The Spanish period of Georgia and South Carolina history, 1566-1702. Athens: University of Georgia Bulletin, XXIII (1923), No. 9b. (23 p.)

Johnson, J. G. "Myths, legends, miracles, and mysteries related by the first historians of Florida." GHQ, VIII (1924), 292-303.

Johnson, J. G. "The Spaniards in northern Georgia during the sixteenth century." GHQ, IX (1925), 159-168.

Johnson, J. G. "The founding of Spanish colonies in Georgia and South Carolina." GHQ, XV (1931), 301-312.

Johnson, J. G. "The colonial southeast, 1732-1763." Boulder, Colo.: University of Colorado Studies, XIX (1932), No. 3, 163-226.

Johnson, C. "A note on absenteeism and pluralism in British West Florida." LHQ, XIX (1936), 196-198.

Jones, C. C., Jr. The history of Georgia. 2 vols. Boston and New York, 1883.

The first edition appeared in Savannah in 1878.

Kenny, M. The Romance of the Floridas. New York, 1934. (395 p.)

Based chiefly in Lowery's classic and other secondary sources; covers mainly the Jesuit period, 1566-1572.

Kimber, E. (ed.). A relation or journal of a late expedition to the gates of St. Augustine on Florida, conducted by the Hon. General James Oglethorpe with a detachment of his regiment, from Georgia [London, 1744]. Boston, 1935. (36 p.)

Knauss, J. O. "William Pope Du Val, pioneer and state builder." FHSQ, XI (1933), 95-139.

William Pope Du Val (1784-1854) was the first civil governor of the territory of Florida.

Knox, D. W. "A forgotten fight in Florida." USNIP, LXII (1936), 507-513.

"An account of the 'spectacular destruction in 1816 of the so-called Negro fort,' located 25 miles up the Apalachicola river in the then Spanish colony of Florida, by a joint military-naval expedition" (Griffin, Writings, 1936, p. 104).

Lanning, J. T. The Spanish missions of Georgia. Chapel Hill: University of North Carolina press, 1935. (321 p.)

An excellent study, based almost exclusively on Spanish primary sources.

Lanning, J. T. The diplomatic history of Georgia: a study of the epoch of Jenkins' ear. Chapel Hill: University of North Carolina press, 1936. (275 p.)

A study of the Anglo-Spanish struggle for Florida, 1721-1763, based on manuscript materials in the archives of England, France, and Spain.

Lanning, J. T. "A descriptive catalogue of some legajos on Georgia in the Spanish archives." GHQ, XIII (1929), 410-421.

Lanning, J. T. "The American colonies in the preliminaries of the War of Jenkins' Ear." CHQ, XI (1927), 129-155.

Lanning, J. T. "Don Miguel Wall and the Spanish attempt against the existence of Carolina and Georgia." NCHR, X (1933), 186-213.

Lanzas, Pedro Torres (ed. and comp.) Relación descriptiva de los mapas, planos . . . de Mexico y Florida existentes en el Archivo General de Indias. 2 vols. Seville, 1900.

La Roncière, C. de. (ed.). La Floride francaise, scene de le vie indienne, peintes en 1564 [par Jacques Le Moyne de Morgues]. Paris, 1928 (139 p.)

Contains maps, an atlas, and 42 plates.

Lawson, J. History of Carolina. London, 1714. (258 p); London, 1718; Raleigh, Va., 1860 (390 p.); Charlotte, N. C., 1903; Richmond, Va., 1937 (259 p.)

Exact description and natural history of that country and a journal of a 1000-mile travel through several nations of Indians.

Le Moyne de Morgues, J. Brevis narratio eorum quae in Florida Americae provincia Gallis acciderunt, secunda in illam Nauigatione, duce Renato de Laudonière classis. Praefecto: Anno M.D. Lxiii. Quae est Secunda Pars Americae.

Account of the Laudonnière expedition to Florida. Its author was an artist who accompanied the expedition and whose drawings were later published by Theodor de Bry (1591). F. B. Perkins published (Boston, 1875) an English translation of Le Moyne's narrative and heliotypes of engravings based on his sketches.

Leonard, I. A. (trans. and ed.). Spanish Approach to Pensacola, 1689-1693. Albuquerque: University of New Mexico press, 1939. (323 p.)

Vol. IX of the Quivira Society Publications. Excellent translation with rich annotations of twenty-one documents dealing with Spain's first attempt to occupy Pensacola Bay. The documents are from Spanish archives.

Leonard, I. A. "Don Andrés de Arriola and the Occupation of Pensacola Bay." New Spain and the Anglo-American West (Los Angeles, 1932), I, 81-106.

Leonard, I. A. (ed. and trans.). "The Spanish re-exploration of the Gulf coast in 1686." MVHR, XXII (1936), 547-557.

Log, kept by Juan Jordan de Reina, of the frigate which the viceroy sent in search of the Bahia del Espiritu Santo (mouth of the Mississippi).

Lockey, J. B. "The Florida intrigues of José Alvarez de Toledo." FHSQ, XII (1934), 145-178.

Deals with the revolutionary activities against Spanish Florida of a Spanish political refugee in the United States, 1811-1816.

Lockey, J. B. (trans. and ed.). "The Saint Augustine Census of 1786." FHSQ, XVIII (1939), 11-31.

Lockey, J. B. "Public education in Spanish St. Augustine." FHSQ, XV (1937), 147-168.

López, A. (ed.). "Cuatro cartas sobre las misiones de la Florida." AIA, I (1914), 255-268.

Prints four letters: two by Fray Francisco Pareja (St. Augustine, March 8, 1599, and San Juan del Puerto. October 12, 1599); one by Fray Baltasar López (St. Augustine. March 8, 1599); one (a report) by Fray Juan Luengo (Madrid, September 22, 1676).

López, Atanasio (ed.). Relación histórica de la Florida, escrita en el siglo XVII [by Fray Gerónimo de Oré], Madrid, 1931.

The first edition of this important *relacion* appeared "in Spain between the years 1617 and 1620," according to Geiger, in the biographical introduction to his English rendition of the *Relación*. See No.

Lovell, C. C. The golden isles of Georgia. Boston, 1932. (300 p.)

Lowery, W. The Spanish settlement within the present limits of the United States: Florida, 1562-1574. New York and London, 1st ed., 1905; 2 ed., 1911. (500 p.)

Heavily documented, covering the Jesuit period of Florida history.

McGrady, E. History of South Carolina under the royal government, 1719-1776. New York, 1889.

McGrady, E. History of South Carolina under the proprietary government, 1670-1719. New York, 1897.

Manning, M. M. "The East Florida papers in the Library of Congress." HAHR, X (1930), 392-397.

Mendelis, L. J. "Colonial Florida." FHSQ, III (1924), 4-15.
Deals with Florida up to the year 1821.

Méndez Arceo, S. "Documentos inéditos que ilustren los obispados Carolense (1519), Tierra Florida (1520) y Yucatán (1561). RHA, No. 9 (Aug., 1940), 31-61.
Eight important documents, in Spanish, with a very scholarly introduction, documents III, IV, and V pertaining to Fray Juan Suarez, bishop-elect of Florida, who came to Florida with the Narváez expedition in 1528.

Mohr, C. H. "St. Francis Barracks, St. Augustine; the Franciscans in Florida." FHSQ, VII (1929), 214-233.

Mowat, C. L. "St. Augustine under the British Flag, 1763-1775." FHQ, XX (1941), 131-150.

O'Daniel, V. F. (ed.). "Carta del obispo de Cuba para su magestad en su real consejo . . . 1606." CHR, II (1917) 442-459.
Official report of canonical visitation, held in Florida by Bishop Altamirano of Cuba in 1606.

O'Daniel, V. F. "The Right Rev. Juan de las Cabezas de Altamirano." CHR, II (1917), 400-414.

Olschki, L. "Ponce de Leon's fountain of youth." HAHR, XXI (1941), 361-385.
A thorough study and appreciation of the ancient legend.

Onís, Luís de. Memoirs upon negotiations between Spain and the United States. Washington, D. C., 1821. (152 p.)

Osterhaut, G. H. "The sites of the French and Spanish forts in Port Royal sound." Huguenot Society of South Carolina, Transactions, XLI (1936), 22-36.

Padgett, J. A. (ed.). "The Constitution of the West Florida Republic." LHQ, XX (1937), 881-894.
Prints the text of the Constitution of October 24, 1810.

Padgett, J. A. (ed.). "The West Florida revolution of 1810, as told in the letters of John Rhea, Fulwar Shipwith, Reuben Kenyer, and others." LHQ, XXI (1938), 76-202.

Padgett, J. A. (ed.). "Commission, orders, and instructions issued to George Johnstone, British governor of West Florida, 1763-1767." LHQ, XXI (1938), 1021-1068.

Padgett, J. A. (ed.). "The difficulties of Andrew Jackson in New Orleans including his later dispute with Fulwar Shipwith, as shown by the document." LHQ, XXI (1938), 367-419.

Padgett, J. A. (ed.). "Minutes of the first session of the assembly of West Florida (November 3, 1766—January 3, 1767)." LHQ, XXII (1939), 311-384, 942-1011; XXIII (1940), 5-77, 353-404.

Pennington, E. L. "Sir John Hawkins in Florida." FHSQ, X (1931), 86-101.

Pennington, E. L. "East Florida in the American revolution, 1775-1778." FHSQ, IX (1930), 24-46.

Pennington, E. L. "The Reverend James Seymour, S.P.G. missionary in Florida." FHSQ, V (1927), 196-201.
A Church of England missionary in Florida in 1783-1784.

Pérez Bustamante, C. "Fr. Bartolomé de Barrientos y su vida y hechos de Pedro Menéndez de Avilés." RLI (1940), 73-88.

A study of the Barrientos report (see No. 216), differing from Lowery's opinion regarding the report.

Phillips, P. L. Notes on the life and works of Bernard Romans. Deland: Florida State Historical Society, 1924. (128 p.)

"This publication places within reach of students the document 'upon which all the detailed geographical knowledge of the Florida Peninsula is based,' the rare map of Florida by Bernard Romans in 1774, reproduced from the copy in the Library of Congress" (Griffin, *Writings,* 1924, p. 83).

Phinney, A. H. "Florida's Spanish missions." FHSQ, IV (1925), 15-21.

Phinney, A. H. "The first Spanish-American war." FHSQ, IV (1926), 114-129.

Phinney, A. H. "The second Spanish-American war." FHSQ, V (1926), 103-111.

Ray, S. H. "Jesuit martyrs in Florida." FHSQ, VI (1928), 182-186.

Reding, K. (trans.). "Letter of Gonzalo Menéndez de Canco, governor of Florida, to Philip II of Spain, June 28, 1600." GHQ, VIII (1924), 215-228.

Deals with the English venture on Roanoke Island.

Reding, K. (trans. and ed.). "Plans for the colonization and defense of Apalache, 1675." GHQ, IX (1925), 169-175.

Reynolds, C. B. Old Saint Augustine. A story of three centuries. 5th ed., St. Augustine, Fla., 1891. (144 p.)

Reynolds, C. B. Fact versus fiction for the new historical St. Augustine. Mountain Lakes, N. J., 1937. (37 p.)

Rivers, W. J. A sketch of the history of South Carolina to the close of the proprietary government by the revolution of 1719. Charleston, S. C., 1856. (470 p.)

Rivers, W. J. A chapter in the early history of South Carolina. Charleston, S. C., 1874. (110 p.)

Robertson, J. A. "The significance of Florida's history." FHSQ, VI (1927), 25-32.

Robertson, J. A. "Notes on early Church government in Spanish Florida." CHR, XVII (1931), 151-174.

Robertson, J. A. (ed.). A history of Florida from the treaty of 1763 to our own times, by Caroline Mays Brevard. 2 vols. Deland: Florida State Historical Society, 1924-1925.

Ross, M. Spanish days in Glynn county. Brunswick, n.d.

Treats of the ancient ruins near the Altamaha-Brunswick Canal and on St. Simons Island, presumed to be what remains of the Franciscan missions.

Ross, M. "The restoration of the Spanish missions in Georgia, 1598-1606." GHQ, X (1926), 171-199.

An excellent study based on Spanish manuscript sources.

Ross, M. "The French on the Savannah, 1605." GHQ, VIII (1924), 167-194.

Deals with encounter between the Spaniards and French corsairs.

Ross, M. "French instrusions and Indian uprisings in Georgia and South Carolina, 1577-1580." GHQ, VII (1923), 251-281.

Based on Spanish primary sources, heavily documented.

Ross, M. "With Pardo and Boyano on the fringes of the Georgia land." GHQ, XIV (1930), 1-19.

Deals with the Pardo-Boyano expedition, 1566-1567. Based on primary sources.

37

Ross, M. "The Spanish settlement of Santa Elena (Port Royal) in 1578." GHQ, IX (1925), 352-379.

Ruidiaz y Caravia, E. La Florida su conquista y colonización por Pedro Menéndez de Avilés. 2 vols. Madrid, 1893.

A valuable storehouse of original sources pertaining to Pedro Menéndez de Avilés and his activities in Florida.

Rutherford, M. L. Georgia—the thirteenth colony. Athens, Ga., 1926. (245 p.)

A history of Georgia, from the early days of discovery and exploration by the Spaniards.

Salley, A. S., Jr. (ed.). Narratives of early Carolina, 1650-1708—Original narratives of early American history. New York, 1911. (388 p.)

Salley, A. S., Jr. (ed.). South Carolina: Journal of the grand council, August 25, 1671—June 24, 1680. Historical Commission of South Carolina, Publications. 2 vols. Columbus, 1907.

Salley, A. S., Jr. "The Spanish settlement of Port Royal, 1565-1586." SCHGM, XXVI (1925), 137-145.

San Miguel, A. de. Relación de los Arabajos que la que la gente de una nao llamada Nra. Señora de la Merced padeció y de algunas cosas que en aquella flota sucedieron. [After 1615.]

The author of this account was Andrés de Sequra, known as Andrés de San Miguel after he entered the Carmelite Order. The events in the Relación, in which the author played a part, occurred twenty years before.

Serrano y Sanz, M. (ed.). Documentos históricos de la Florida y la Louisiana. Siglos XVI al XVIII. Madrid, 1912. (466 p.)

A valuable collection of original documents, most of which pertain to West Florida.

Shea, J. G. "Ancient Florida"—Narrative and critical history of America, Justin Winsor (ed.). II (London, 1886), 231-298.

Important for the critical notes and comments by the editor on the bibliography of early Florida. The essay by Shea covers the period from 1513 to 1574.

Shores, V. L. "The ruins of fort San Luís near Tallahassee." FHSQ, VI (1927), 111-116.

Siebert, W. H. "Slavery and white servitude in East Florida, 1726-1776." FHSQ, X (1932), 3-23, 139-161.

Siebert, W. H. "Some Church history of St. Augustine during the Spanish régime." FHSQ, IX (1930), 117-123.

Siebert, W. H. "The departure of the Spaniards and other groups from East Florida, 1763-1764." FHSQ, XIX (1940), 145-154.

Based on Spanish accounts, showing how, at the time of the cession, most of the inhabitants left Florida, chiefly for Havana.

Siebert, W. H. "East Florida as a refuge of southern loyalists, 1774-1775." Worcester, Mass.: American Antiquarian Society, Proceedings, n.s. XXXVII (1928), pt. 2, 226-246.

Siebert, W. H. Loyalists in East Florida (1774-1785). 2 vols. Deland, Fla., 1929.

Vol. I contains the author's narrative and Vol. II the records of Loyalist claims for losses of property.

South Carolina Historical Society Collections. 5 vols. Charleston, S. C., 1857-1897.

Steck, F. B. " 'Captain John Smith' in Florida." FH, XXIII (1936), 81-83, 104-107.

The story of Juan Ortíz, based on the account in Garcilaso de la Vega's La Florida del Inca.

Steck, F. B. "The first school in the United States." FR, XXXVIII (1931), 3-4.

Stevens, W. B. A history of Georgia from its first discovery by Europeans to the adoption of the present constitution in MDCCXCVIII. 2 vols. I, New York, 1847; II, Philadelphia, 1859.

Stock, L. F. (ed.). Proceedings and debates of the British Parliaments respecting North America. 4 vols. Washington, D. C.: Carnegie Institution of Washington, 1924-1937.
> Contains background material on Anglo-Spanish relations in Florida, late seventeenth and early eighteenth centuries.

Stone, D. "The relationship of Florida archaeology to that of Middle America." FHSQ, XVII (1939), 211-218.

Stork, W. A description of East Florida with a journal kept by John Bartram of Philadelphia . . . London, 1st ed., 1765; London, 3rd ed., 1769. (40 p.)
> Important for the flora and fauna of East Florida; contains Bartram's journal. See No.

Swanton, J R. Early history of the Creek Indians and their neighbors. Washington, D. C.: Government Printing Office, 1922. (492 p.)
> A standard work with six valuable charts.

Vargas Ugarte, Rubén (ed.). "First Jesuit mission in Florida." RSUSCHS, XXV (1935), 59-148.
> Twenty documents on the history of the Jesuits in Florida covering the four years (1568-1572).

Vigil, C. M. Noticias biográfico-genealógicas de Pedro Menéndez de Avilés, primer adelantado y conquistador de la Florida. Avilés, 1892. (201 p.)

Wallace, D. D. ["Pardo's route through South Carolina in 1567"]. HAHR, XVI (1936), 447-450.
> A discussion, with photograph, of what may be an inscription left by the Pardo expedition in South Carolina in 1567.

Warren, H. G. "Pensacola and the filibusters, 1816-1817." LHQ, XXI (1938), 806-922.

Webber, M. J. (ed.). "Josiah Smith's diary, 1780-1781." SCHM, XXXIII (1932), 1-28, 79-116, 197-207, 281-289.
> Smith was an exile from Charleston, S. C., to St. Augustine during the British occupation of Charleston.

Wenhold, L. L. (trans.). A 17th century letter of Gabriel Díaz Calderón, Bishop of Cuba, describing the Indians and Indian missions of Florida. Washington, D. C.: Smithsonian Institution, Miscellaneous Collections, vol. 95, No. 16. 1936. (14 p.)

Whitaker, A. P. (trans. and ed.). Documents relating to the commercial policy of Spain in the Floridas. Deland: Florida State Historical Society, Publications, No. 10, 1931. (277 p.)
> A well-edited, with Spanish text and English translation, collection of thirty important documents from the public archives of Spain, from 1778-1808.

Whitaker, A. P. "Spain and the Cherokee Indians, 1783-1798." NCHR, IV (1927), 252-269.
> Shows that Spain's policy was to protect the Indians against American aggression in the Floridas; based on primary Spanish sources.

Williamson, H. History of North Carolina. 2 vols. Philadelphia, 1812.

Willcox, Major C. DeWitt. (trans). [Letters of Governor Montiano of Florida relating to the siege of St. Augustine.] Savannah: Georgia Historical Society, Collections, VII, pt. 1, 1909.
> The letters cover the period from 1737-1741.

DeRenne, W. J. (trans.). [Official Spanish account of the attack on Georgia.] Savannah: Georgia Historical Society, Collections, VII, pt. 2, 1913.
> The documents are copies from the originals in the Archivo general de las Indias, Seville, Spain.

Wright, I. A. "Spanish policy toward Virginia, 1606-1612; Jamestown, Ecija and John Cook of the Mayflower." AHR, XXV (1920), 448-479.

Includes the text of some important Spanish documents bearing on the early Anglo-Spanish relations in Florida.

Wyllys, R. K. "The filibusters of Amelia Island." GHQ, XII (1928), 297-325.

Discusses in how far the filibusters brought about the occupation of East and West Florida, 1817-1818, and the Spanish-American wars of independence caused the southward expansion of the United States.

Wyllys, R. K. "The East Florida revolution of 1812-1814." HAHR, IX (1929), 415-445.

Deals with the filibustering in East Florida from the United States incidental to the Spanish-American wars of independence.

Zubillaga, F. La missión jesuítica de la Florida, 1566-1572. Rome: Institutum Historicum S. I., 1941. vol. 1. (473 p.)

This is the first volume (others to follow), based in large part on hitherto unpublished documents.

Zubillaga, F. "Pedro Martínez, 1533-1566; la primera sangre jesuita en las misiones norteamericanas." AHSI, VII (1938), 30-53.

IV. LOUISIANA, 1763-1803

Abbey, K. T. "Peter Chester's defense of the Mississippi after the Willing raid." MVHR, XXII (1935), 17-32.

Story of an incident of Anglo-American rivalry in 1778.

Aiton, A. S. "The diplomacy of the Louisiana cession." AHR, XXXVI (1931), 701-720.

Aiton, A. S. "A letter in answer to Dr. Stenberg's article." LHQ, XIX (1936), 1075-1077.

Ambler, C. H. History of transportation in the Ohio Valley. Glendale, Calif., 1931. (465 p.)

Barbe-Marbois, F. Marquis de. Histoire de la Louisiane, et de la cession de cette colonie par la France aux États-Unis de l'Amérique Septentrionale. Paris, 1829. (485 p.)

The author was secretary of the French legation in Washington, 1779-1795.

Baudier, R. The Catholic Church in Louisiana. New Orleans, priv. print., 1939. (605 p.)

Covers the entire history from earliest explorations to modern transition period.

Beard, C. A. The Aaron Burr conspiracy, by W. F. McCaleb. New York, 1936. (318 p.)

Bemis, S. F. "The renewal memoranda of 1782 on western boundaries and some comments on the French historian Doniol." Worcester, Mass.: American Antiquarian Society. Proceedings, LXVII (1938), 15-92.

Binger, H. "The Louisiana Purchase and our title west of the Rockies."

Bispam, C. W. "Contest for ecclesiastical supremacy in the valley of the Mississippi, 1763-1803." LHQ, I (1917), 154-189.

Bjork, D. K. "Alexander O'Reilly and the Spanish occupation of Louisiana, 1769-1770." New Spain and the Anglo-American West, Los Angeles, 1932, I, 165-182.

Bjork, D. K. (ed.). "Documents relating to Alexander O'Reilly and an expedition sent out by him from New Orleans to Natchitoches, 1769 - 1770." LHQ, VII (1924), 20-39.

Deals with a phase of the establishment of Spanish authority in Louisiana after its cession by France.

Bjork, D. K. (trans. and ed.). "Documents relating to the establishment of schools in Louisiana, 1771." MVHR, XI (1925). 561-569.

Bloom, L. B. "The death of Jacques d'Eglise," NMHR, II (1927), 369-379.

D'Eglise was a French trader active in upper Missouri during the Spanish period; later went to New Mexico where he was murdered by a Spaniard in 1809.

Bolton, H. E. "General James Wilkinson as adviser to Emperor Iturbide." HAHR, I (1918), 163-180.

Bolton, H. E. (ed.). Athanase de Mézières and the Louisiana-Texas frontier, 1768-1780. 2 vols. Cleveland, 1914.

"Documents published for the first time, from the original Spanish and French manuscripts, chiefly in the archives of Mexico and Spain; translated into English; edited and annotated by Herbert Eugene Bolton.

Bonham, M. L., Jr. "A postscript to the founding of New Madrid." MVHR, XIX (1932), 408-409.

Concerning Savelle's study on the same topic. (See No. 603.)

Bonham, M. L., Jr. "The Spanish flag in Louisiana." HAHR, I (1918), 457-460.

Breazele, P. "Uncle Tom's Cabin and 'The Spanish post of the Adaias'." LHQ, VII (1924), 304-307.

Brooks, P. C. "Spain's farewell to Louisiana, 1803-1821." MVHR, XXVII (1940), 29-43.

Burson, C. M. The stewardship of don Estéban Miró, 1782-1792. New Orleans, 1940. (327 p.)
"A study of Louisiana based largely on documents in New Orleans." Miró was governor of Louisiana during the Spanish régime. Valuable for history of social conditions.

Campbell, E. F. "New Orleans at the time of the Louisiana Purchase." GR, XI (1921), 414-425.

Carpenter, E. H., Jr. "Arsène Lacarrière Latour." HAHR, XVIII (1938), 221-227.
Latour was a secret agent of Spain immediately following the Purchase of Louisiana (1803). "The Spanish officials," to quote Carpenter, "considered Latour a valuable and trustworthy agent, and ordinarily relied on his word" in shaping their policy after the Louisiana Purchase.

Brooks, P. C. "Pichardo's treatise and the 'Adams-Onis treaty." HAHR, XV (1935), 94-97.

Caughey, J. W. "The Panis mission to Pensacola." HAHR, X (1930), 480-489.

Caughey, J. W. "The Natchez rebellion of 1781 and its aftermath." LHQ, XVI (1933), 57-83.
Story of the Indian uprising against Spanish authority.

Caughey, J. W. "Bernardo de Gálvez and the English smugglers on the Mississippi, 1777." HAHR, XII (1932), 46-48.
Study of illicit British trade in Spanish Louisiana and efforts of Governor Gálvez to stop it.

Caughey, J. W. Bernardo de Gálvez in Louisiana, 1776-1783. Berkeley: University of California press, 1934. (290 p.)
An important and scholarly study.

Chambers, H. E. A history of Louisiana. 3 vols. Chicago, 1925.
Vol. I is a comprehensive history of Louisiana; vols. II and III contain biographical material.

Champigny, Colonel Chevalier de. La Louisiane ensanglentée. London, 1773. (32 p.)

Champigny, Colonel Chevalier de. État present de la Louisiane, avec toutes les particularités de cette Province d'Amérique. La Heye, 1776. (147 p.)

Charlevoix, F. X. Histoire et description general de la Nouvelle-France, avec le journal historique d'un voyage fait por ordre du roi dans l'Amérique Septentrionale. 4 vols. Paris, 1744.
Of particular value for the Franco-Spanish war of 1719-1721, for the history of which the author had access to official documents. Contains extremely valuable charts. English translation by John Gilmary Shea, 6 vols., New York, 1866-1872, with critical notes.

Clark, D. Proofs of the corruption of General James Wilkinson. Philadelphia, 1809. (199 p.)
". . . a remarkably accurate account of Wilkinson's dealings with the Spaniards. All that the book lacks is what the title claims to give —the proofs. These were in the Spanish archives, and are still there," A. P. Whitaker, *The Mississippi Question*, 1795-1803, p. 288.

Colliard, B. "Rummaging through old parish records. Historical sketch of the parish of Opelousas, La., 1770-1903." StL CHR, III (1921), 14-38.
First half of the article deals with the records prior to 1800.

Collins, L. M. "The activities of the missionaries among the Cherokees." GHQ, VI (1922), 285-322.

Corbitt, D. C. "Spanish ambition in the Illinois country, 1782." Springfield: Journal, Illinois State Historical Society, XXIX (1936), 92-93.
Includes a letter (Nov. 20, 1782) from Governor Miró to Bernardo de Gálvez.

42

Corbitt, D. C. "James Colbert and the Spanish claims to the east bank of the Mississippi." MVHR, XXIV (1938), 457-472.

Cox, I. J. "The Louisiana-Texas frontier during the Burr conspiracy." MVHR, X (1923), 274-284.

Cox, I. J. The West Florida controversy. Baltimore, 1918. (699 p.)

Cox, I. J. "Hispanic-American phases of the 'Burr Conspiracy'." HAHR, XII (1932), 145-175.

Craighead, E. From Mobile's past. Mobile, 1925. (255 p.)
> Contains "sketches of memorable people and events" in the history of Mobile, Ala.

Craighead, E. Mobile, fact and tradition. Mobile, 1930. (373 p.)
> Tells of "noteworthy people and events" in the history of Mobile, Ala.

Darby, W. Geographical description of Louisiana. Philadelphia, 1816. (270 p.)

Dart, H. P. (ed.). "The oath of allegiance to Spain." LHQ, IV (1921), 205-215.
> Copies of the oath which was taken by inhabitants of Spanish Illinois and by those of Pointe Coupée and "Fausse River" in 1769.

Dart, H. P. "Spain and France at Biloxi in 1699." LHQ, VII (1924), 480-484.

Dart, H. P. (ed.), "Civil procedure in Louisiana under the Spanish regime as illustrated in Loppinot's case, 1774." LHQ, XII (1929), 33-120.
> The documents (40-120) concern the loss of a slave.

Dart, H. P. (ed.). "Fire protection in New Orleans in Unsaga's time." LHQ, IV (1921), 201-204.

Dart, H. P. "The adventures of Denis Brand, the first printer of Louisiana, 1764-1773." LHQ, XIV (1931), 349-360.

Dart, H. P. (ed.). "Public education in New Orleans in 1800." LHQ, XI (1928), 241-242.
> A Frenchman, Luis Francisco Lafort, desires to open a school for higher education in New Orleans.

Dart, H. P. and L. L. Porteous (ed. and trans.). "Account of the credit and debit of the funds of the city of New Orleans for the year 1789." LHQ, XIX (1936), 584-594.

Dart, H. P. and L. L. Porteous (eds.). "The Spanish procedure in Louisiana in 1800 for licensing doctors and surgeons." LHQ, XIV (1931), 204-207.

Dart, H. P. (ed.). "A Louisiana conventional mortgage of the Spanish colonial period." LHQ, VI (1923), 255-258.

Dart, H. P. "A Louisiana indigo plantation on Bayou Teche, 1773." LHQ, IX (1926), 565-589.

Dart, H. P. (ed.). "A sale of real property in Louisiana in 1769." LHQ, XXI (1938), 674-676.

Dart, H. P. (ed.). "Almonester's will." LHQ, VI (1923), 21-34.
> The will was drawn up in 1794.

Dart, H. P. (ed.). "A criminal trial before the Superior Council of Louisiana, May, 1747." LHQ, XIII (1930), 367-390.

Dart, H. P. (ed.). "Trial of Mary Glass for murder, 1780." LHQ, VI (1923), 591-654.

Dart, H. P. (ed.). "A lawsuit in the court of the governor at New Orleans involving land in Opelousas, 1764." LHQ, XII (1929), 533-554.

Dart, H. P. "A twelve year lawsuit in New Orleans during the Spanish régime (1781-1792)." LHQ, XVII (1934), 294-305.

Dart, H. P. (ed.). "A murder case tried in New Orleans in 1773." LHQ, XXII (1939), 623-641.

Dart, H. P. (ed.). "Jackson and the Louisiana Legislature, 1815." LHQ, IX (1926), 221-280.

Reprint of a rare pamphlet, published in New Orleans in 1815, containing report of the Louisiana legislature on the closure of its sessions by General Jackson on December 28, 1814.

Debouchel, V. Histoire de la Louisiane depuis les premières découvertes jusqu' en 1840. New Orleans, 1840. (197 p.)

DeLanglez, J. The French Jesuits in Lower Louisiana, 1700-1763. Washington, D. C.: The Catholic University of America press, 1935. (547 p.)

Document. "The capture of Baton Rouge by Gálvez, September 21st, 1779." LHQ, XII (1929), 255-265.

Reprint of reports from the *London Gazette* of April 1, 1780, giving the English version of the capture of Baton Rouge by the Spaniards.

Document. "Sanitary conditions in New Orleans under the Spanish régime, 1799-1800." LHQ, XV (1932), 610-617.

Document. "Memoire des habitants et negotians de la Louisiane, sur l'événement du 29. Octobre 1768." Boston: Massachusetts Historical Society, Photostat Reproductions, American Series, No. 250.

The memorial, drawn up by Denis Brand, states the grievances and defends the revolt of the colonists and expulsion of the Spanish governor, Antonio de Ulloa.

Document. Recollections of Thomas Beckwith — Glimpses of the past. St. Louis, Mo.: Missouri Historical Society, II (1935), 32-42.

Reminiscences of life in Missouri during the middle of the 18th century.

Document. [Spanish officers and soldiers in Louisiana, 1770-1792.] New Orleans: Louisiana Society, Sons of the American Revolution, Year Book (1921), 94-106.

Document. State papers and correspondence bearing upon the purchase of the territory of Louisiana. Washington, D. C., 1903.

Document. "Statutes of the Diocese of Louisiana and the Floridas, issued by Rt. Rev. Luís Ignatius Peñalver y Cárdenas in 1795." USCHM (1887), 417-442.

Prints the Spanish text and an English translation.

Ellicott, A. The journal of Andrew Ellicott, late commissioner on behalf of the United States during 1796-1800: for determining the boundary between the United States and the possessions of His Catholic Majesty in America . . . Philadelphia, 1803. (450 p.)

The volume contains also "occasional remarks on the situation, soil, rivers, natural productions, and diseases of the different countries on the Ohio, Mississippi and Gulf of Mexico, with 6 maps comprehending the Ohio, Mississippi from mouth of Ohio to Gulf, the whole of West Florida, part of East Florida. To which is added an appendix, containing all the astronomical observations made use of for determining the boundary."

Espinosa, J. M. "Spanish Louisiana and the West: the economic significance of the Ste. Genevieve district." MHR, XXXII (1938), 287-297.

Faye, S. "Consuls of Spain in New Orleans, 1804-1821." LHQ, XXI (1938), 677-684.

Faye, S. (ed.). "The garden of Fray Antonio de Sedella." LHQ, XXI (1938), 1068-1074.

Faye, S. (ed.). "The schism of 1805 in New Orleans." LHQ, XXII (1939), 98-141.

Faye, S. (ed.). "Louis Declouet's Memorial to the Spanish government, December 7, 1814." LHQ, XII (1939), 795-818.

Faye, S. "The great stroke of Pierre Laffite." LHQ, XXIII (1940), 733-826.

Faye, S. "The Altamira case." LHQ, XXV (1942), 5-23.

Fortier, A. History of Louisiana. 4 vols. New York, 1904.

Franz, A. Die kolonisation des Mississippitales bis zum ausgange der französischen herrschaft. Leipzig, 1906. (464 p.)

French, B. (ed.). Historical collections of Louisiana and Florida. New York and Philadelphia, ser. I, 5 vols. ser. II, 2 vols.

Garrett, J. K. "Letters and Documents. Doctor John Sibley and the Louisiana-Texas frontier, 1803 - 1814." SHQ, XLV (1942), 286 - 301, 378 - 382; XLVI (1942), 83-84.

Garretson, O. A. "Iowa and the Spanish pioneers." IJHP, XXX (1932), 395-403.

Gassler, F. L. "Pere Antoine, supreme officer of the holy inquisition of Cartagena, in Louisiana." CHR, II (1922), 59-63.

Gayarré, C. Histoire de la Louisiane. 2 vols. New Orleans, 1845-1847.

The English edition, *History of Louisiana,* New York, 1851-1854, comprises 5 volumes. A vast amount of new source material has been uncovered since C. K. Adams wrote: "The work [of Gayarré] has a standard value, and is a reservoir from which every student of French and Spanish occupation [in Louisiana] may draw supplies. The author's style is spirited, and, though he does not rise into the highest realm of historical merit, his discriminations are, for the most part, just, and his conclusions such as will be approved" (*Manual of Historical Literature,* New York, 1882, p. 561).

Goodspeed, W. A. The province and the states: a history of the province of Louisiana under France and Spain and of the territories and states of the United States formed therefrom. . . . 7 vols. Madison, Wis., 1904.

Goodwin, G. L. "The Louisiana territory from 1682-1803." LHQ, III (1920), 5-25.

Gregg, K. L. "The Boonslick road in St. Charles county." MHR, XXVII (1933), 307 - 314; XXVIII (1934), 9-16.

An account of a road, which first began (1769) as a trail over which early settlers traveled.

Hackett, C. W. "Policy of the Spanish crown regarding French encroachments from Louisiana, 1721-1762." Los Angeles: New Spain and the Anglo-American West, Los Angeles, 1932, I, 107-145.

Hamilton, P. J. Colonial Mobile. New York, 1897. (446 p.)

Hardin, J. F. "Don Juan Filhiol and the founding of Fort Miro, the modern Monroe, Louisiana." LHQ, XX (1937), 463-485.

A study of one of the first Spanish forts in Louisiana, based on original sources.

Hart, S. H. and A. B. Hulbert (eds.). Zebulon Pike's Arkansaw journal. Denver, Colo., 1932. (142 p.)

Hay, T. R. "General James Wilkinson—the last phase." LHQ, XIX (1936), 407-435.

Hay, T. R. and M. R. Werner. The admirable trumpeter: a biography of General James Wilkinson. New York, 1941. (383 p.)

Heinrich, Pierre. La Louisiane sous la compagnie des Indes, 1717-1731. Paris, n.d. (298 p.)

Hill, W. H. (ed.). "Rev. James Maxwell, missionary at St. Genevieve, by Firmin A. Rozier." USCHM (1887), 283-286.

Holmes, W. C. "The exalted enterprise (the Mississippi question: the Louisiana answer)." LHQ, XXIII (1940), 78-106.

Hosmer, J. K. The history of the Louisiana Purchase. New York, 1902. (230 p.)

45

Hough, E. The Mississippi bubble. Indianapolis, 1902. (452 p.)

Houck, L. The Spanish régime in Missouri. 2 vols. Chicago, 1909.

Kendall, J. S. "Piracy in the Gulf of Mexico, 1816-1823." LHQ, VIII (1925), 341-368.

King, A. R. Social and economic life in Spanish Louisiana, 1763-1783. Urbana: University of Illinois, 1931.

King, G. New Orleans: the place and the people. New York, 1895. (404 p.)

Kinnaird, L. (ed.). "Clark-Leyba papers." AHR, XLI (1935), 92-112.

Twenty-five letters (1778-1779), mostly between George Rogers Clark and the Spanish commander of the Illinois country, Fernando de Leyba.

Kinnaird, L. "The Spanish expedition against Fort St. Joseph in 1781: a new interpretation." MVHR, XIX (1932), 173-191.

Kinnaird, L. "American penetration into Spanish Louisiana." Los Angeles: New Spain and the Anglo-American West, Los Angeles, 1932, I, 211-237.

Lafargue, A. "A reign of twenty days—Pierre Clement de Laussat." LHQ, VIII (1925), 398-410.

Lafargue, L. "The Louisiana Purchase: the French viewpoint." LHQ, XXIII (1940), 107-117.

Shows the influence of the French Revolution and of French encyclopedists in the retrocession of Louisiana from Spain to France.

La Harpe, B. de. Journal historique de l'établissement des Francais a la Louisiane. New Orleans, 1831. (412 p.)

Morrow, E. L. and L. Morrow (eds.) The life and exploits of Gasparilla, last of the buccaneers, by Edwin D. Lambright. Tampa, Fla., 1936. (221 p.)

A biographical account of José Gasparilla (1756-1821), Spanish pirate who made his headquarters on the Florida coast, and a historical account of "Ye mystic krewe of Gasparilla," the organization which has charge of the Gasparilla carnival which has been celebrated in Tampa each year since 1904. See Griffin, *Writings,* 1936, p. 160.

Leonard, I. A. (ed. and trans.). "The Spanish re-exploration of the Gulf coast in 1686." MVHR, XXII (1936), 547-557.

"The log of Juan Jordan de Reina on the expedition commanded by Barroto and Romero.

Le Page du Pratz. Histoire de la Louisiane. 3 vols. Paris, 1758.

Le Page arrived in Louisiana in 1718. The *Histoire* "contenant la decouverte de ce vaste pays; sa description géographique; un voyage dans les terres; l'histoire naturelle; les moeurs, coûtumes et religion des naturels, avec leurs origines; deux voyages dansle nord du Nouveau Mexique, dont un jusqu'à la Mer du Sud; ornée de deux cartes et 40 planches en taille douce" (description sub-title).

Lewis, A. (trans. and ed.). "Fort Panmure, 1779, as related by Juan Delavillebeuvre to Bernardo de Gálvez." MVHR, XVIII (1932), 541-548.

An interesting description of conditions at a Spanish frontier post in the Southwest during the American Revolution.

Lewis, A. "Du Tisne's expedition into Oklahoma, 1719." CO, III (1925), 319-323.

Lewis, A. "Oklahoma as a part of the Spanish dominion, 1763-1803." CO, II (1924), 45-58.

Lewis, A. "La Harpe's first expedition in Oklahoma, 1718-1719." CO, II (1924), 331-349.

Liljegren, E. R. "Jacobinism in Spanish Louisiana, 1792-1797." LHQ, XXII (1939), 46-97.

Lyon, E. W. Louisiana in French diplomacy, 1759-1804. Norman: University of Oklahoma press, 1934. (268 p.)

McCutcheon, R. P. "Books and booksellers in New Orleans, 1730-1830." LHQ, XX (1937), 616-618.

McCutcheon, R. P. "Libraries in New Orleans, 1771-1833." LHQ, XX (1937), 152-158.

McMurtrie, D. C. The pioneer printer of New Orleans. Chicago: Eyncouth press, 1930. (17 p.)

Denis Brand, official printer in Louisiana from 1764-1770.

Margry, Pierre. Mémoires et documents pour servir a l'histoire des origines Françaises des pays d'outre-mer; découvertes et établissements des Français dans l'ouest et dans le sud d'Amérique Septentrionale, 1614-1754. 6 vols. Paris, 1879-1888.

The volumes should be consulted for the Franco-Spanish conflict in Louisiana and Texas, though Margry's transcripts are not always reliable.

Marshall, T. M. A history of the western boundary of the Louisiana Purchase. Berkeley: University of California press, 1914. (266 p.)

Martin, F. X. The history of Louisiana from the earliest period. 2 vols. New Orleans, 1827.

Based for the most part on Charlevoix and Le Page du Pratz.

Mason, E. C. "The march of the Spaniards across Illinois." MAH, XV (1886), 457-470.

Molyneux, P. "A romantic borderland: Texas-Louisiana frontier, a region of stirring events and glamorous tradition." BM, I (1928), 272-300.

Morgan, W. T. "English fear of 'encirclement' in the seventeenth century." CanHR, X (1929), 4-22.

Rivalry of France, Spain, and England in the Mississippi valley.

Murphy, L. E. "Beginnings of Methodism in Missouri, 1798-1824." MHR, XXI (1927), 370-394.

Nachbin, J. "Spain's report of the war with the British in Louisiana." LHQ, XV (1932), 468-481.

Nasatir, A. P. and E. R. Liljegren. "Materials relating to the history of the Mississippi valley. From the minutes of the Spanish Supreme Council of State, 1787 - 1797." LHQ, XXI (1938), 5-75.

Nasatir, A. P. "Jacques Clamorgan: colonial promoter of the northern border of New Spain." NMHR, XVII (1942), 101-112.

Nasatir, A. P. "The formation of the Missouri Company." MHR, XXV (1930), 10-22.

Nasatir, A. P. "Anglo-Spanish rivalry on the Upper Missouri." MVHR, XVI (1929), 359-382; 507-530.

Deals with the rivalry of British and Spanish traders during the last decade of Spanish rule in Louisiana.

Nasatir, A. P. (ed.). "John Evans, explorer and surveyor." MHR, XXV (1931), 219-239, 432-460, 585-608.

Contains twenty-eight important documents, 1792-1798, from the Archivo general de Indias.

Nasatir, A. P. "The Anglo-Spanish frontier on the upper Mississippi, 1786 - 1796." IJHP, XXIX (1931), 155-232.

Nasatir, A. P. "Anglo-Spanish rivalry in the Iowa country, 1797-1798." IJHP, XXVIII (1930), 337-389.

Nasatir, A. P. "Ducharme's invasion of Missouri, an incident in the Anglo-Spanish rivalry for the Indian trade of upper Louisiana." MHR, XXIV (1929), 3-25.

Nasatir, A. P. "St. Louis during the British attack of 1780." Los Angeles: New Spain and the Anglo-American West, Los Angeles, 1932, I, 239-261.

Nasatir, A. P. "The Anglo-Spanish frontier in the Illinois country during the American Revolution, 1779-1783." Springfield: Journal, Illinois State Historical Society, XXI (1928), 291-358.

Nugent, H. P. (trans.). Historical memoir of the war in West Florida and Louisiana in 1814-1816, by Major A. Lacarrière Latour. 2 vols. Philadelphia, 1916.

Padgett, J. A. (ed.). "The ancestry of Edward Livingston of Louisiana: the Livingston family." LHQ, XIX (1936), 900-937.

Padgett, J. A. (ed.). "Letters of Edward Livingston to Presidents of the United States." LHQ, XIX (1936) 938-963; XX (1937), 58-136.

Padgett, J. A. (ed.). "A decree for Louisiana issued by the Baron de Carondelet, June 1, 1795." LHQ, XX (1937), 590-605.

Padgett, J. A. "Constitution of the West Florida republic." LHQ, XX (1937), 881-894.

Padgett, J. A. (ed.). "Some documents relating to the Batture controversy in New Orleans." LHQ, XXIII (1940), 679-732.

Pease, T. C. "The Mississippi boundary of 1763: a reappraisal of responsibility." AHR, XL (1935), 278-286.

The author "tries to make Bute the villain of the piece" (Hanke, *Handbook*, 1935, p. 92).

Pelzer, L. "Economic factors in the acquisition of Louisiana." Lincoln, Neb.: Proceedings, Mississippi Valley Historical Association, VI (1912), 109-128.

Perrin de Lac, M. Voyage dans les deux Louisianes en 1801, 1802, 1803. Lyon, 1805 (479 p.)

A German translation by K. L. Mueller was published in Leipzig in 1807.

Phelps, A. Louisiana: a record of expansion. New York, 1905. (412 p.)

Pierson, W. W. "The establishment and early functioning of the Intendencia of Cuba." Chapel Hill: James Sprunt Historical Publications, University of North Carolina, XIX (1927), 74-133.

Pike, Z. M. An account of expeditions . . . to the sources of the Arkansaw. Philadelphia, 1810. (227 p.)

Pike, Z. M. Exploratory travels through the western territory of North America . . . performed in the years 1805-07, by order of the Government of the United States. Denver, 1889. (394 p.)

Comprises "a voyage from St. Louis, on the Mississippi to the source of that river, and a journey through the interior of Louisiana and the northeastern provinces of New Spain . . ."

Porteous, L. L. (ed.). "Index to the Spanish judicial records of Louisiana." LHQ, VI (1923) and volumes following.

The valuable Index, the first instalment of which appeared in Vol. VI (1923), ran continuously in the issues of the *Louisiana Historical Quarterly*.

Porteous, L. L. "Torture in Spanish criminal procedure in Louisiana, 1771." LHQ, VIII (1925), 5-22.

Deals, on the basis of an official record, with the "criminal proceedings . . . to find the aggressor who killed Juan Baptiste Cesaire Lebreton, on the night of May 21, 1771."

Porteous, L. L. "A suit for debt in the governor's court, New Orleans, 1771." LHQ, VIII (1925), 240-247.

Porteous, L. L. "Trial of Pablo Rocheblave before Governor Unzaga, 1771." LHQ, VIII (1925), 372-381.

Porteous, L. L. (ed.). "Marriage contracts of the Spanish period in Louisiana." LHQ, IX (1926), 385-397.

From the Spanish judicial archives of 1770, 1773, and 1779.

Porteous, L. L. (trans.). "Procedure to obtain the Spanish intendant's consent to the private sale of an American vessel in New Orleans, 1803." LHQ, X (1927), 185-191.

Porteous, L. L. (trans.). "Governor Carondelet's levee ordinance of 1792." LHQ, X (1927), 513-516.

Porteous, L. L. and H. P. Dart (eds.). "A judicial auction in New Orleans, 1772." LHQ, XI (1929), 32-38.

Porteous, L. L. (trans.). "Marine survey of schooner Charlotte and sale of said vessel at auction, Nov. 24, 1777." LHQ, XIII (1930), 230-234.

Porteous, L. L. and H. P. Dart (eds.). "Documents covering the prosecution of Denis Brand, regidor of the Cabildo for the crime of running away from Louisiana." LHQ, XIV (1931), 361-382.

Porteous, L. L. "The Gri-Gri case." LHQ, XVII (1934), 48-63.
The case was tried in 1773.

Posey,. W. B. The development of Methodism in the old Southwest, 1783-1824. Tuscoloosa, Ala., 1933. (151 p.)

Renaut, F. P. La question de la Louisiane. Paris, 1918. (242 p.)

Renaut, F. P. La pacte de famille et l'Amérique: la politique coloniale franco-espagnole de 1760 a 1792. Paris, 1942. (458 p.)

Riley, F. L. "Spanish policy in Mississippi after the treaty of San Lorenzo." Report, American Historical Association, 1897. Washington, D. C. (1898), 177-192.

Riley, M. L. "The development of education in Louisiana prior to statehood." LHQ, XIX (1936), 595-634.
The study includes conditions during the Spanish regime.

Robertson, J. A. (ed. and trans.). Louisiana under the rule of Spain, France, and the United States, 1785-1807. Cleveland, 1911. 2 vols.
A collection of documents, some of them previously unpublished.

Robertson, J. A. "Spanish correspondence concerning the American Revolution." HAHR, I (1918), 299-316.
Letters (1776, 1777, 1778) by Unzaga and Gálvez, governors of Louisiana, concerning the American Revolution.

Rodríguez Casado, V. Primeros años de dominación española en la Luisiana. Madrid: Consejo Superior de Investigaciones Científicas. Inst. Gonzalo Fernández de Oviedo, 1942. (497 p.)
From the antecedents of the Treaty of Fontainbleau (1763) to the end of the régime of Governor O'Reilly (1770) of Louisiana.

Rojas, L. A. de. "The great fire of 1788 in New Orleans." LHQ, XX (1937), 578-589.

Rojas, L. A. de. "A consequence of the Louisiana Purchase." LHQ, XXI (1938), 362-366.
Increase of mining, commerce, and agriculture in New Spain, due to closer relations with the United States.

Rothensteiner, J. "The old St. Louis Calvary." StLCHR, III (1921), 39-49.
Notes on the ancient site of Calvary cemetery (1792 and 1795).

Rothensteiner, J. "Historical sketch of Catholic New Madrid." StLCHR, IV (1922), 113-129.
Traces the history of the New Madrid parish from its earliest times to the year 1804.

Rothensteiner, J. "Father James Maxwell of Ste. Genevieve." StLCHR, IV (1922), 142-154.
Activities of Father Maxwell in Spanish Louisiana and discussion of the so-called "Maxwell Claim."

Savelle, M. "The founding of New Madrid, Missouri." MVHR, XIX (1932), 30-56.
Tells of the founding of New Madrid in 1789 by George Morgan and party from New Jersey.

Shepherd, W. R. "The cession of Louisiana to Spain." PSQ, XIX (1904), 439-458.

49

Siebert, W. H. "Spanish and French privateering in southern waters, July, 1762 to March, 1763." GHR, XVI (1932), 163-178.

Silver, J. W. (ed.). "General Edmund P. Gaines and the protection of the southwestern frontiers." LHQ, XX (1937), 183-191.
A series of original documents.

Stenberg, R. R. "The boundaries of the Louisiana Purchase." HAHR, XIV (1934), 32-64.

Stenberg, R. R. "The western boundary of Louisiana, 1762-1803." SHQ, XXXV (1931), 95-108.

Stenberg, R. R. "The Louisiana cession and the family compact." LHQ, XIX (1936), 204-209.

Stenberg, R. R. "Napoleon's cession of Louisiana: a suggestion." LHQ, XXI (1938), 354-361.
The writer suggests that Napoleon's plan was to cede the Floridas to the United States; instead, he had to sell Louisiana, Spain refusing to cede the Floridas to him.

Stoddard, A. Sketches of Louisiana. Philadelphia, 1812. (488 p.)
A description of New Orleans at the end of the Spanish period.

Swanton, J. R. Indian tribes of the lower Mississippi Valley and adjacent coast of the Gulf of Mexico. Washington, D. C.: Government Printing Office, 1911. (387 p.)

Sugar, L. "Following the Spanish trail across the 'neutral territory' in Louisiana." LHQ, X (1927), 86-93.

Swartzlow, R. J. "The early history of lead mining in Missouri." MHR, XXVIII (1934), 184 - 194, 287 - 295; XXIX (1935), 27-34, 109-114, 195-205.
An account of mining in Missouri from 1700 to 1820.

Teggard, F. J. "Capture of St. Joseph, Michigan, by the Spaniards in 1781." MHR, V (1911), 214-228.

Thomas, A. B. "The massacre of the Villasur expedition at the forks of the Platte river, Aug. 12, 1720." NH, VII (1924), 68-81.

Thomas, A. B. "Spanish activities in the lower Mississippi Valley, 1513 - 1698." LHQ, XXII (1939), 3-12.
An interpretative summary, emphasizing the De Soto expedition.

Viles, J. "Population and extent of settlement in Missouri before 1804." MHR, V (1911), 189-213.

Villiers du Terrage, M. de. Les dernières années de la Louisiane francaise. Paris, 1904. (468 p.)

Villiers du Terrage, M. de. Histoire de la fondation de la Nouvelle Orleans (1717 - 1722). Paris, 1917. (129 p.)

Villiers du Terrage, M. de. "New chapter in Nebraska history." NH, VI (1923), 1-31.
Deals with the Villasur expedition of 1720.

Violette, E. M. "Spanish land claims in Missouri." St. Louis, Mo.: Washington University Studies, Humanistic series, VIII, no. 2, 167-200.

Vogel, C. L. The Capuchins in French Louisiana, 1722-1766. Washington, D. C.: The Catholic University of America press, 1928. (201 p.)

Whitaker, A. P. The Spanish-American frontier: 1783-1795. Boston and New York, 1927. (255 p.)
Deals with "the westward movement and the Spanish retreat in the Mississippi valley" (sub-title). An excellent study showing how the western frontier influenced diplomacy between Spain and the United States.

Whitaker, A. P. "Spain and the Cherokee Indians, 1783-98." NCHR, IV (1927), 252-269.

Discusses Spain's policy of protecting the Indians against American aggression and securing their friendship.

Whitaker, A. P. The Mississippi question, 1795-1803: a study in trade, politics, and diplomacy. New York, 1934. (342 p.)

A masterly study, heavily documented.

Whitaker, A. P. "Louisiana in the treaty of Basel." JMH, VIII (1936), 1-26.

Deals with the Franco-Spanish treaty negotiations (1795) to determine "the reason for the failure of France's determined effort to recover Louisiana."

Whitaker, A. P. "The retrocession of Louisiana in Spanish policy." AHR, XXXIX (1934), 454-476.

Whitaker, A. P. "Harry Innes and the Spanish intrigue, 1794-1795." MVHR, XV (1928), 236-248.

Whitaker, A. P. "Alexander McGillivray, 1783-1793." NCHR, V (1928), 181-203, 289-309.

Whitaker, A. P. "France and the American deposit at New Orleans." HAHR, XI (1931), 485-502.

Whitaker, A. P. "Antonio de Ulloa." HAHR, XV (1935) 155-194.

Biographical sketch of Ulloa, historiographer of Spanish America, naval officer, and governor of Louisiana, 1766-1779.

Whitaker, A. P. "The commerce of Louisiana and the Floridas at the end of the eighteenth century." HAHR, VIII (1928), 190-203.

Whitaker, A. P. "James Wilkinson's first descent to New Orleans in 1787." HAHR, VIII (1928), 82-97.

Documents with introduction on the question: "How did Wilkinson succeed where others had failed?" (p. 82).

Wilgus, A. C. "Spanish-American patriot activity along the Gulf of the United States, 1811-1822." LHQ, VIII (1925), 193-215.

Deals with Spanish-Americans in Louisiana and Texas supporting the revolutions against Spain in violation of the neutrality of the United States.

Winston, J. E. "Notes on the economic history of New Orleans, 1803 - 1836." MVHR, XI (1924), 200-226.

Winston, J. E. "New Orleans and the Texas Revolution." LHQ, X (1927), 317-354.

Winston, J. E. "How the Louisiana Purchase was financed." LHQ, XII (1929), 189-237.

Winston, J. E. "The cause and result of the revolution of 1768 in Louisiana." LHQ, XV (1932), 181-213.

Winston, J. E. "New Orleans newspapers and the Texas question, 1835-1837." LHQ, XXXVI (1932), 109-129.

Winston, J. E. "Louisiana and the annexation of Texas." LHQ, XIX (1936), 89-118.

Wood, M. "Life in New Orleans in the Spanish period." LHQ, XXII (1939), 642-709.

Winston, J. E. (ed.). "A faithful picture of the political situation in New Orleans at the close of the last and the beginning of the present year, 1807." LHQ, XI (1928), 359-433.

Reprint of the Boston, 1808, edition of a pamphlet published in New Orleans in 1807 or 1808. The author of the pamphlet was either Edward Livingston or Judge James Workman.

V. TEXAS, 1689-1836

Abel, A. H. "Mexico as a field for systematic British colonization, 1839." SHQ, XXX (1926), 63-67.

Proposed opposition in the British House of Commons to the Republic of Texas.

Abel, A. H. (ed.). A report from Natchitoches in 1807. New York: Museum of the American Indian, Indian Notes and Monographs, 1922. (102 p.)

Agreda, Sor María de Jesús de. Autenticidad de la Mística Ciudad de Dios y biografía de su autora. Barcelona, 1914. (544 p.)

The question of María de Agreda's visits among the Jumanos Indians of western Texas is treated in chapter 9 of Treatise Two and chapter 4 of Treatise Eight (pp. 127-138 and 416-437).

Alessio Robles, V. Coahuila y Texas en la época colonial. Mexico, 1938. (754 p.)

A splendid, authoritative study, heavily documented, with a rich bibliography.

Alessio Robles, V. Saltillo en la historia y en la leyenda. Mexico, 1934. (254 p.)

Alessio Robles, V. Monterrey en la historia y en la leyenda. Mexico, 1936. (266 p.)

The story of the city of Monterrey, Mexico, from 1581 to the present day.

Alessio Robles, V. La primera imprenta en las provincias internas de oriente: Texas, Tamaulipas, Nuero León y Coahuila. Mexico, 1939. (79 p.)

Alessio Robles, V. (ed.). "El derrotero de la entrada a Texas del gobernador de Coahuila sargento mayor Martín de Alarcón." UdeM, V (1932), 48-69 (1933), 217-239.

The diary of Francisco Céliz, chaplain of the expedition, April 9, 1718, to February 6, 1719.

Alessio Robles, V. (ed.). Viaje de indios y diario del Nuevo Mexico, por el rev. fray Juan Augustín de Morfi. Mexico, D.F., 1935. (306 p.)

Second edition of Morfi's work with a bibliographical introduction and annotations by the editor. The first edition appeared in 1856.

Almonte, J. N. Noticias estadísticas sobre Tejas. Mexico, 1835. (96 p.)

Contains diary of journey from Natchitoches to Mexico City across Texas and a description of economic conditions, the Indians, and the geography of Texas on the eve of the establishment of the republic.

Allen, H. E. "The Parilla expedition to the Red River in 1759." SHQ, XLIII (1939), 53-71.

Arricivita, Juan Domingo. Crónica seráfica y apostólica del Colegio de Propaganda Fide de la Santa Cruz de Querétaro en la Neuva España, dedicada el Santísimo Patriarca el Señor San Joseph. Segunda Parte. Mexico, 1792. (605 p.)

A continuation of Espinosa's Cronica.

Atkinson, M. J. The Texas Indians. San Antonio, Tex., 1935. (345 p.)

Austin, M. A. "The municipal government of San Fernando de Bejar, 1730-1800." SHQ, VIII (1905), 277-253.

Baker, K. W. "Nacogdoches," SR, XXI (1935), 1-14.

Bancroft, H. H. History of the North Mexican States and Texas. 2 vols. San Francisco, 1884-1889.

Valuable for references to authorities.

Barker, E. C. (ed.). The Austin papers. 2 vols. Washington, D. C.: Government Printing Office, 1924.

Barker, E. C. The life of Stephen F. Austin, founder of Texas, 1793 - 1836. Nashville and Dallas, 1925. (551 p.)

Barker, E. C. Mexico and Texas, 1821 - 1835. Dallas, 1928. (167 p.)
The lectures of Professor Barker on the causes of the Texas Revolution.

Barker, E. C. "Difficulties of a Mexican revenue officer in Texas." SHQ, IV (1901), 190-202.

Barker, E. C. "Funeral of the heroes of the Alamo." SHQ, V (1902), 69-70.

Barker, E. C. "The government of Austin's colony, 1821-1831." SHQ, XXI (1918), 223-252.

Barker, E. C. "The journal of the Permanent Council. October 11-27, 1835." SHQ, VII (1904), 249-278.

Barker, E. C. "Land speculation as a cause of the Texas Revolution." SHQ, X (1907), 76-95.

Barker, E. C. "Minutes of the Ayuntamiento of San Felipe de Austin, 1828-1832." SHQ, XXI (1918), and volumes following.
These valuable records ran continuously in The Southwestern Historical Quarterly to volume XXIV (1921).

Barker, E. C. "Notes on early Texas newspapers, 1819-1836." SHQ, XXI (127-144).

Barker, E. C. "The San Jacinto campaign." SHQ, IV (1901), 237-245.

Barker, E. C. "Stephen F. Austin." SHQ,. XXII (1919), 1-17.

Barker, E. C. (ed.). "Some Fannin correspondence." SHQ, VII (1904), 318-325.

Barker, E. C. "Stephen F. Austin and the independence of Texas." SHQ, XIII (1910), 257-284.

Barker, E. C. "The Texan declaration of causes for taking up arms against Mexico." SHQ, XV (1912), 173-185.

Barker, E. C. "The Texan revolutionary army." SHQ, IX (1906), 227-261.

Barker, E. C. "Descriptions of Texas by Stephen F. Austin." SHQ, XXVIII (1925), 98-121.

Bennett, M. S. "The battle of Gonzales, the 'Lexington' of the Texas Revolution." SHQ, II (1899), 313-316.

Beckner, L. (ed.). "A letter from Texas." FCHQ, X (1936), 116-119.
The letter was written by S. Perry Williams, a Kentuckian, in 1836; has bearing on Fannin's surrender to Santa Anna at Goliad in 1836.

Biesele, R. L. "Prince Solm's trip to Texas, 1844-1845." SHQ, XL (1936), 1-25.

Binkley, W. C. (ed.). Official correspondence of the Texas Revolution, 1835-1836. 2 vols. New York, 1936.

Blake, R. B. "Location of the early Spanish missions and presidio in Nacogdoches County." SHQ, XLI (1938), 212-224.

Bolton, H. E. Texas in the middle eighteenth century. Berkeley: University of California press, 1915. (501 p.)

Bolton, H. E. "The beginnings of Mission Nuestra Señora del Refugio." SHQ, XIX (1916), 400-404.

Bolton, H. E. "The founding of Mission Rosario: a chapter in the history of the Gulf coast." SHQ, X (1906), 113-139.

Bolton, H. E. "The founding of the missions on the San Gabriel River, 1745-1749." SHQ, XVII (1914), 323-378.

Bolton, H. E. "The Jumano Indians in Texas, 1650-1771." SHQ, XV (1911), 66-84.

Bolton, H. E. "The location of La Salle's colony on the Gulf of Mexico," MVHR, II (1915), 165-182.

Bolton, H. E. "Massanet or Manzanet." SHQ, X (1907), 101.

Bolton, H. E. "The native tribes about the East Texas missions." SHQ, XI (1908), 249-276.

Bolton, H. E. "New light on Manuel Lisa and the Spanish fur trade." SHQ, XVII (1913), 61-66.

Bolton, H. E. "Notes on Clark's 'The beginnings of Texas'." SHQ, XII (1908), 148-158.

Bolton, H. E. "The old stone fort at Nacogdoches." SHQ, IX (1906), 283-285.

Bolton, H. E. "Records of the mission of Nuestra Señora del Refugio." SHQ, XIV (1911), 164-166.

Bolton, H. E. "Some materials for southwestern history in the Archivo General de Mexico." SHQ, VI (1903), 103-112; VII (1904), 196-213.

Bolton, H. E. "The Spanish abandonment and reoccupation of East Texas, 1773-1779." SHQ, IX (1906), 67-137.

Bolton, H. E. "Spanish activities on the Lower Trinity River, 1746 - 1771." SHQ, XVI (1913), 339-377.

Bolton, H. E. "Spanish mission records at San Antonio." SHQ, X (1907), 297-307.

Bolton, H. E. "The Spanish occupation of Texas, 1519-1690." SHQ, XVI (1912), 1-26.

Bolton, H. E. "A correction." SHQ, XVI (1913), 225.

Bolton, H. E. (ed. and trans.). "Tienda de Cuervo's Inspección of Laredo, 1757." SHQ, VI (1903), 187-203.

Bonilla, Antonio. Breve compendio de la historia de Texas, 1722. Mexico, D. F.: Archivo General de la Nación, Boletín, IX (1938), 677-729.
First publication in Spanish of Bonilla's report to Viceroy Bucareli on Texan affairs from 1685 to 1772. An English translation was published by E. H. West in 1904 in *The Southwestern Historical Quarterly.*

Boyle, A. A. "Reminiscences of the Texas Revolution." SHQ, XIII (1910), 285-291.

Brondo, J. P. Nuevo León, Mexico. Mexico, 1938. (387 p.)
Deals with the colonial history of Nuevo León.

Brooks, C. M. Texas missions: their romance and architecture. Dallas, Tex., 1936. (154 p.)

Brooks, P. C. "Pichardo's treaties and the Adams-Onís treaty." HAHR, XV (1935), 94-99.
Discusses the influence of Pichardo's treaties on the treaty of 1819.

Buckley, E. C. "The Aguayo expedition into Texas and Louisiana, 1719-1722." SHQ, XV (1912), 1-65.

Bugbee, L. G. "The name Alamo." SHQ, II (1899), 245-247.

Bugbee, L. G. "The real St. Denis." SHQ, I (1898), 266-281.

Butterfield, J. C. Men of Alamo, Goliad, and San Jacinto. San Antonio, Tex., 1936. (46 p.)

Callahan, E. H. "The Franciscan missions of San Antonio." OW, XXVIII (1908), 21-49.
Deals with the missions in and around San Antonio.

Casis, L. M. (trans.). "Carta de don Damián Mansanet a Don Carlos de Sigüenza sobre el descubrimiento de la Bahía del Espíritu Santo." SHQ, II (1899), 253-312.
An English translation of this important document with a facsimile reproduction of the original. In vol. III of SHQ (p. 70) a correction is published.

Castañeda, C. E. "Silent years of Texas history." SHQ, XXXVIII (1935), 122-134.

Castañeda, C. E. (trans.). "Statistical report on Texas by Juan N. Almonte." SHQ, XXVIII (1925), 177-222.
Report of Colonel Almonte to Secretary of War in Mexico.

Castañeda, C. E. (trans.). "A trip to Texas in 1828, José María Sánchez." SHQ, XXIX (1926), 249-288.

Castañeda, C. E. Three manuscript maps of Texas by Stephen F. Austin; with biographical and bibliographical notes. Austin, 1930. (55 p.)

Casteñeda, C. E. "Customs and legends of Texas Indians." M-A, III (1931), 48-56.

Castañeda, C. E. "Communications between Santa Fé and San Antonio in the eighteenth century." TGM, V (1941), 17-38; also reprint. (38 p.)

Castañeda, C. E. (trans. and ed.). The Mexican side of the Texas Revolution (1836). Dallas, Tex., 1928. (391 p.)
A series of reports "by the chief participants, General Antonio López de Santa Anna, D. Ramón Martínez Caro . . . General Vicente Filisola, General José Urrea, General José María Tornel" (subtitle).

Castañeda, C. E. A report on the Spanish archives in San Antonio, Texas. San Antonio, 1937. (167 p.)

Castañeda, C. E. "Alonso de León, precursor de Tejas." SegCIHA (1938), II, 142-162.

Castañeda, C. E. "A chapter in frontier history." SR, XXVIII (1942), 31-52; also reprint. (21 p.)
Texas and especially San Antonio and vicinity on the eve and at the outbreak of the revolution in Mexico in 1810.

Castañeda, C. E. "Earliest Catholic activities in Texas." CHR, XVII (1931), 278-295; also Preliminary Studies of the Texas Catholic Historical Society (Austin, 1931). I, No. 8. (18 p.)

Castañeda, C. E. (trans.). History of Texas, 1673-1779, by Fray Juan Augustín Morfi. 2 vols. Albuquerque, N. M., 1935.
A Quivira Society publication, No. 6, with a biography of Morfi and critical annotations by the translator and editor.

Castañeda, C. E. and F. C. Chabot. Excerpts from the Memorias [of Fray Juan Augustín Morfi] for the history of the province of Texas. San Antonio, priv. print., 1932. (85 p.)
"A translation of those parts of the Memorias which particularly concern the various Indians of the province of Texas" (subtitle); from the photostat copy of the Memorias (462 folios) in the University of Texas Library, the original being in the Library of Congress, Washington, D. C.

Castañeda, C. E. Our Catholic heritage in Texas. 4 vols. Austin, Texas, 1936-1939.
Contains: Vol. I, The founding of Texas, 1519-1693; Vol. II, The winning of Texas, 1693-1731; Vol. III, The mission era: the missions at work, 1731-1776; Vol. IV, The mission era: the passing of the missions, 1762-1782. The fifth and last volume of the colonial series is in progress. An authoritative work, based in large measure on hitherto unpublished primary sources, written with the lay reader in view. Enriched with extensive biobliographies of primary and secondary sources.

Chabot, F. C. The Alamo, altar of Texas liberty. San Antonio, 1931. (141 p.)

Chabot, F. C. The Alamo. San Antonio, 1935. (53 p.)

Chabot, F. C. Mission La Purísima Concepción. San Antonio, 1935. (51 p.)

Chabot, F. C. San Antonio and its beginnings, 1691-1731. San Antonio, 1936. (99 p.)
Also an earlier (1931) and larger (130 pages) edition of this work.

56

Chabot, F. C. (ed.). Memoirs by Antonio Menchaca. San Antonio, 1937. (31 p.)
Covers events from 1800 to 1835.

Chabot, F. C. (ed.) Texas in 1811. The Las Casas and Sambrano revolutions. San Antonio, 1941. (162 p.)
Deals with the activities of Captain Juan Las Casas in the Texan Revolution.

Chapman, J. "San Antonio." SR, XXII (1936). 16-40.

Clark, R. C. "The beginnings of Texas—Fort St. Louis and Mission San Francisco de los Tejas." SHQ, V (1902), 171-205.

Clark, R. C. "The beginnings of Texas, 1684-1718." Austin: Bulletin, University of Texas, 1907, no. 98. (94 p.)

Clark, R. C. "Louis Juchereau de St. Denis and the re-establishment of the Tejas missions." SHQ, VI (1903), 1-26.

Cleaves, W. S. "Lorenzo de Zavala in Texas." SHQ, XXXVI, (1933), 29-40.

Coopwood, B. "Concerning Saint Denis." SHQ, II (1899). 97-98.

Coopwood, B. "Notes on the history of La Bahía del Espíritu Santo." SHQ, II (1899). 162-169.

Corner, W. (comp. and ed.). San Antonio de Bejar: a guide and history. San Antonio, 1890. (166 p.)

Corner, W. "John Crittenden Duval: The last survivor of the Goliad massacre." SHQ, I (1898), 47-67.

Cox, I. J. "The early settlers of San Fernando." SHQ, V (1902), 142-160.

Cox, I. J. "Father Edmond John Peter Schmitt." SHQ, V (1902), 206-211.

Cox, I. J. "Educational efforts in San Fernando de Bejar." SHQ, VI (1903), 27-63.

Cox, I. J. "The founding of the first Texas municipality." SHQ, II (1899), 217-226.

Cox, I. J. "A correction by Edmond J. P. Schmitt." SHQ, III (1900), 285.

Cox, I. J. "The Louisiana-Texas frontier." SHQ, X (1907), 1-75; XVII (1913), 1-42, 140-187.

Cox, I. J. "The southwestern boundary of Texas." SHQ, VI (1903), 81-102.

Cox, I. J. (ed.). The journeys of René Cavelier Sieur de la Salle. 2 vols. New York, 1905.
Contains accounts by La Salle "faithful Lieutenant, Henri de Tonty; his famous colleagues, Fathers Zenobius Membre, Louis Hennepin and Anastasius Douay; his early biographer, Father Christian LeClercq; his trusted subordinate, Henri Joutel; and his brother, Jean Cavelier; together with Memoirs, commissions, etc." (subtitle).

Crocket, G. L. Two centuries in east Texas; a history of San Augustine county and surrounding territory from 1685 to the present time. Dallas, Tex., 1932. (372 p.)
Deals with the Texas-Louisiana frontier, Franco-Spanish and Mexican-American rivalry and the early statehood of Texas to the Civil War.

Crockett, D. The adventures of Davy Crockett [1786-1836] told mostly by himself. New York and London, 1934. (258 p.)
Contains the autobiography of David Crockett, written in 1834, and (pp. 135-260) his career in Texas.

Coy, O. C. "The last expedition of Josiah Gregg." SHQ, XX (1917), 41-49.

Cunningham, C. H. "The residencia in the Spanish colonies." SHQ, XXI (1918), 253-278.

57

Dabbs, J. A. (trans.). "The Texas missions in 1785." M-A XXII (1940), 38-58; also Preliminary Studies of the Texas Catholic Historical Society (Austin, Texas), III, No. 6 (24 p.)

Dabney, L. E. "Louis Aury, the first governor of Texas under the Mexican republic." SHQ, XLII (1938), 108-116.

Davis, M. E. M. "Louis Juchereau De Saint Denis." SHQ, I (1898), 305-306.

Dealey, J. Q. "The Spanish source of the Mexican constitution of 1824." SHQ, III (1899), 161-169.

Delanglez, J. The journal of Jean Cavelier: the account of a survivor of La Salle's Texas expedition, 1684-1688. Chicago: Loyola University press, 1938. (179 p.)

Dienst, A. "Contemporary poetry of the Texan revolution." SHQ, XXI (1917), 156-184.

Dixon, S. H. and L. W. Kemp. The heroes of San Jacinto. Houston, Tex., 1932. (462 p.)
Biographical sketches of soldiers in the battle against Santa Anna with (pp. 1-34) an historical introduction.

Dobie, J. F. "The first cattle in Texas, and the southwest progenitors of the longhorns." SHQ, XLII (1939), 171-197.

Dobie, J. F. "Stories in Texas names." SHQ, XXI (1936), 125-136, 278-294.

Document. Derrotero de la expedición en la provincia de Texas, nuevo reino de Philipinas . . . Año de 1722. Boston: Massachusetts Historical Society, Photostat Reproductions, American Series, No. 17. 29 numbered leaves.
Juan Antonio de la Peña's account of the Aguayo expedition of 1722.

Document. Constitución política del estado libre de Coahuila y Texas. Leona Vicario (Saltillo), 1829.

Document. "Exploration and settlement in Texas." Bolton, H. E.: Spanish Exploration in the Southwest, 1542-1706. 281-423.
Contains translation of the documents relating to the Bosque-Larios expedition, the Mendoza-López expedition, and the León-Massanet expeditions.

Document. "Texas, four miles from headquarters: a letter to his parents, April 10, 1836" by G. A. Giddings. SHQ, IX (1905), 63-64.

Donoghue, D. "Explorations of Albert Pike in Texas." SHQ, XXXIX (1935), 135-138.
Traces journey through Texas in 1832.

Dorsey, G. A. Traditions of the Caddo. Washington, D. C.: Carnegie Institution of Washington, No. 41, 1905.

Dunn, W. E. "The Apache mission on the San Sabá River: its founding and failure." SHQ, XVII (1914), 379-414.

Dunn, W. E. "Apache relations in Texas, 1718-1750." SHQ, XIV (1911), 198-274.

Dunn, W. E. "The founding of Nuestra Señora del Refugio, the last Spanish mission in Texas." SHQ, XXV (1921), 174-184.

Dunn, W. E. "The Spanish search for La Salle's colony on the Bay of Espíritu Santo, 1685-1689." SHQ, XIX (1916), 323-369.

Dunn, W. E. "Missionary activities among the eastern Apaches." SHQ, XV (1911), 186-200.

Dunn, W. E. "History of Natchitoches." LHQ, III (1920), 26-56.

Eby, F. The development of education in Texas. New York, 1925. (354 p.)

Edward, D. B. History of Texas. Cincinnati, 1836. (336 p.)

Included are several rare and early public documents, among them the two sessional constitutions of 1832 and 1833 and the Mexican constitution of 1824.

Engelhardt, Z. "Missionary labors of the Franciscans among the Indians of the early days— Texas." FH, II (1914), 384-386 and following to Vol. V, 425-428.

For this serial the author used not only the ancient Spanish chronicles, but also the current results of investigations by other scholars in the field of Texas history.

Espinosa, Isidro Felis de. Chrónica apostólico, y seráphica de todos los colegios de Propaganda Fide de esta Nueva-España. Mexico, 1746. (781 p.)

A standard work with rich materials on the Franciscans in Texas by one who himself was active in Texas as missionary. The work was continued by Juan Domingo Arricivita.

Espinosa, Isidro Felis de. El peregrino septentrional atlante delineado en la exemplarissima vida del venerable Padre F. Antonio Margíl de Jesús. Mexico, 1737. (460 p.)

Fitzmorris, Sister M. Angela. Four decades of Catholicism in Texas, 1820-1860. Washington, D. C.: Catholic University of America press, 1926. (109 p.)

Flores D. J. (ed.). Viaje a Texas en 1828-1829. Mexico, 1939. (79 p.)

Spanish text of the diary kept by José María Sánchez, member of the commission sent by the Mexican government to gather information regarding the boundary between Mexico and the United States.

Foik, P. J. Captain Dom Domingo Ramon's diary of his expedition into Texas in 1716. Preliminary Studies of the Texas Catholic Historical Society, Austin, II 1933), No. 5. (23 p.)

Folmer, H. "De Bellisle on the Texas coast." SHQ, XLIV (1941), 225-231.

A discussion of the location of St. Bernard Bay.

Forrestal, P. P. (trans.). The Solís diary of 1767. Preliminary Studies of the Texas Catholic Historical Society, Austin, I (1931), No. VI. (42 p.)

Forrestal, P. P. (trans.). "Peña's diary of the Aguayo expedition." RSUSCHS, XXIV (1934); also Preliminary Studies of the Texas Catholic Historical Society (Austin), II (1935), No. 7. (68 p.)

Frejes. F. Historia breve de la conquista de los estados independientes del imperio Mexicano. Mexico, 1839; 2nd ed., Guadalajara, 1878. (277 p.)

Fray Francisco Frejes was official chronicler of the Franciscan Colegio De Nuestra Señora de Guadalupe de Zacatecas. The *Historia Breve* contains important data, notably on missionary activities in northern Mexico and in Texas, New Mexico and Lower California.

Friend, L. "Old Spanish fort." Year Book, West Texas Historical Association (Abeline), XVI (1941), 5-10.

Gambrell, H. P. Mirabeau Buonaparte Lamar, troubadour and crusader. Dallas, Texas, 1934. (317 p.)

García, Bartholomé. Manual para administrar lós santos sacramentos de penitencia, eucharistía, extrema unción, y matrimonio. Mexico, 1760. (88 p.)

This missionary manual by one who labored in the Texas missions is important for study of social conditions in middle-eighteenth century Texas.

García, Genaro (ed.). Historia de Nuevo León con noticias sobre Coahuila, Tejas, Nuevo Mexico, por el capitán Alonso de León, un autor anónimo, y el general Fernando Sánchez de Zamora. Mexico, 1909. (400 p.)

Garrett, J. K. "The first newspaper of Texas: Gaceta de Texas," SHQ, XL (1937), 200-215.

Garrett, J. K. "The first constitution of Texas, April 17, 1813," SHQ, XL (1937) 290-308.

Garrett, J. K. (trans.). "Gaceta de Texas: translation of the first number." SHQ, XLII (1938), 21-27.

Garrett, J. K. Green flag over Texas: a story of the last years of Spain in Texas. New York and Dallas, 1939. (279 p.)

Garrison, G. P. "Question concerning convention of 1833." SHQ, III (1899), 153.

Garrison, G. P. Texas, a contest of civilization. Boston, 1903. (320 p.)

Garrison, G. P. Diplomatic correspondence of Republic of Texas. 3 vols. Washington, D. C., 1907.

Garver, L. "Benjamin Rush Milam." SHQ, XXXVIII (1934), 79-121, 177-202.

Glover, W. B. "A history of the Caddo Indians." LHQ, XVIII (1935), 872-946.

Gómez, M. Compendio de historia antigua completa de Coahuila y Texas. Saltillo, 1927.

Graham, P. (ed.). "Mirabeau B. Lamar's first trip to Texas." SR, XXI (1936), 369-389.

Grayson, P. W. "The release of Stephen F. Austin from prison." SHQ, XIV (1910), 155-163.

Greer, J. K. "The committee on the Texas declaration of independence." SHQ, XXX (1927), 239-251; XXXI (1927), 33-49, 130-149.

Greer, J. K. "Journal of Ammon Underwood, 1834-1838." SHQ, XXII (1928), 124-151.

Hackett, C. W. "Visitador Rivera's criticism of Aguayo's work in Texas." HAHR, XVI (1936), 162-172.

Haggard, J. V. "Epidemic cholera in Texas, 1833-1834." SHQ, XL (1937), 216-230.

Haggard, J. V. "The counter revolution of Bexar, 1811." SHQ, XLIII (1940), 222-235.

Haggard, J. V. (trans.). "Letters and documents: Spain's Indian policy in Texas." SHQ, XLVI (1941), 202-208; XLVI (1942), 75-82.

Harris, H. W. "Almonte's inspection of Texas in 1834." SHQ, XLI (1938), 195-211.

Hatcher, M. A. "Myths of the Tejas Indians." Austin: Texas Folk-lore Society, Publications, VI (1927), 107-118.

Hatcher, M. A. "Conditions in Texas affecting the colonization problem, 1795-1801." SHQ, XXV (1921), 81-97.

Hatcher, M. A. and P. J. Foik (trans. and ed.). The expedition of Domingo Terande los Rios into Texas. Austin: Preliminary Studies of the Texas Catholic Historical Society, II (1932), No. 1. (67 p.)

Hatcher, M. A. (trans.). "Description of the Tejas or Asinai Indians, 1691-1722." SHQ, XXX (1926), 206-218, 283-304; XXXI (1927), 50-62, 150-180. Translation of three important documents: (1) letter of Fray Francisco de Casañas to the Viceroy of Mexico, August 15, 1691; (2) extract from letter of Fray Francisco Hidalgo to Fray Isidro Cassos, Nov. 20, 1710, and his letter to the Viceroy of Mexico, Nov. 4, 1716; (3) account by Fray Isidro Felis de Espinosa on the Asinai Indians and their allies.

Hatcher, M. A. (trans.) "Joaquín de Arredondo's report of the battle of the Medina, August 18, 1813." SHQ, XI (1908), 220-236.

Hatcher, M. A. (trans.). "Letters of Antonio Martínez, the last Spanish governor of Texas, 1817-1822." SHQ, XXXIX (1934), 66-72, 139-147, 228-238, 327-332.

Hatcher, M. A. "The Louisiana background of the colonization of Texas, 1763-1803." SHQ, XXIV (1920), 169-194.

Hatcher, M. A. "The municipal government of San Fernando de Bejar, 1730-1800." SHQ, VIII (1905), 277-352.

Hatcher, M. A. "Plan of Stephen F. Austin for an institute of modern languages at San Felipe de Austin." SHQ, XII (1909), 231-239.

Hatcher, M. A. (trans.). "Texas in 1820." SHQ, XXIII (1919), 47-68.

Hatcher, M. A. The opening of Texas to foreign settlement, 1801-1821. Austin: University of Texas, Bulletin (1927), No. 2417. (368 p.)

Hatcher, M. A. and E. L. Kelly (eds.). "Tadeo Ortíz de Ayala and the colonization of Texas, 1822 - 1833." SHQ, XXXII (1928), 74-86, 152-164, 222-251, 311-343.

Held, J. A. Religion a factor in building Texas. San Antonio, 1940. (167 p.)
Deals more particularly with the establishment and progress of the non-Catholic denominations in Texas.

Henderson, M. V. "Minor empresario contracts for the colonization of Texas, 1825-1834." SHQ. XXXI (1928), 295-324; XXXII (1929), 1-28.

Heusinger, E. W. Early explorations and mission establishments in Texas. San Antonio, Tex., 1936. (222 p.)
A popular rather than critical account of the Texas mission era; readable but not always reliable.

Higgs, C. D. "Spanish contacts with the Ais (Indian River) Country." FHSQ, XXI (1942), 25-39.

Hill, L. F. José de Escandón and the founding of Nuevo Santander: a study in Spanish colonization. Columbus: Ohio State University press, 1926. (149 p.)
Traces the development of Mexico's northeastern frontier.

Hodge, F. W. "The Jumano Indians." Worcester, Mass.: Proceedings, American Antiquarian Society, XX (1910), 249-268.

Hoffman, F. L. "The Mesquía diary of the Alarcón expedition." SHQ, XLI (1938), 312-323.

Hoffman, F. L. (trans.) Diary of the Alarcón expedition into Texas, 1718-1719, by Fray Francisco de Céliz. Los Angeles, 1935. (124 p.)
This is Vol. V of the Quivira Society publications.

Holley, M. A. Texas. Austin, Tex., 1935. (410 p.)
This is a facsimile reproduction of the original edition, published in Lexington, Ky., in 1836.

Howren, A. "Causes and origin of the decree of April 6, 1930." SHQ, XVI (1913), 378-422.

Hughes, A. E. The beginnings of Spanish settlement in the El Paso district. Berkeley: University of California Publications in History, I (1914), No. 3 pp. 295-392.

Hutchins, W. A. "The community acequia: its origin and development." SHQ, XXXI (1928), 261-284.
A valuable study, tracing the history of the "ditch" irrigation system in the Spanish Southwest.

Jeffries, C. "The lights of the Alamo." SHQ, XLVI (1942), 1-8.
Explains why Santa Ana was victorious in the Battle of the Alamo, 1836.

John, G. O'Brien. (ed.). Texas history, an outline. New York, 1935. (238 p.)

A corrected abridgement of Yoakum's work with new matter from "original letters and documents in the editor's personal collection" (Foreword).

Jones, A. H. (ed.). "The storming of San Antonio, December 6-9, 1835." SHQ, X (1906), 181-182.

Reprint of a letter written at the time.

Kirwin, J. M. (ed.). Diamond jubilee, 1847-1922, of the Diocese of Galveston and St. Mary's Cathedral. Galveston, 1922. (131 p.)

Kress, M. K. (trans.). "Diary of a visit of inspection of the Texas missions made by Fray Gaspár José de Solís in the year 1767-68." SHQ, XXXV (1921), 28-76.

With an introduction by M. A. Austin.

Lawrence, E. "Mexican trade between Santa Fé and Los Angeles, 1830-1847." CHSQ, X (1931), 27-39.

León, A. de. Historia de Nuevo León con noticias sobre Coahuila, Texas y Nuevo México. Mexico, 1909. (400 p.)

Lewis, A. Along the Arkansas. Dallas, Tex., 1932. (297 p.)

"History of the lower Arkansas river country, now Oklahoma and Arkansas, from 1536 to 1800. Based on published narratives and documents, and on the manuscript reports of Spanish colonial officials of the late 18th century" (Griffin, *Writings*, 1932, p. 70).

Looscan, A. B. "Harris county, 1822 - 1845." SHQ, XVIII (1915), 195-207, 261-286, 399-409; XIX (1916), 37-64.

Looscan, A. B. "Letter from a 'Mier' prisoner to his mother." SHQ, V (1901), 66-68.

Looscan, A. B. "Manuel Frederick Gibenrath, the German drummer of Goliad." SHQ, XIV (1910), 166-168.

Looscan, A. B. "Micajah Autry, a soldier of the Alamo." SHQ, XIV (1911), 315-324.

Looscan, A. B. "The old fort at Anahuac." SHQ, II (1898), 21-28.

Looscan, A. B. "The old fort on the San Sabá river as seen by Dr. Ferdinand Roemer in 1847." SHQ, V (1901), 137-141.

Looscan, A. B. "The old Mexican fort at Velasco." SHQ, I (1898), 282-284.

McCaleb, W. F. "The attitude of the Spanish in Texas towards the Indians." SHQ, I (1898), 126-127.

McCaleb, W. F. "The first period of the Gutiérrez-Magee expedition." SHQ, IV (1901), 218-229.

McCaleb, W. F. "Some obscure points in the mission period of Texas history." SHQ, I (1898), 216-225.

McClintock, W. A. "Journal of a trip through Texas and northern Mexico in 1846-1847." SHQ, XXXIV (1930), 20-37, 141-158, 231-256.

McGrath, Sister Paul. Political nativism in Texas, 1825-1860. Washington, D. C.: Catholic University of America press, 1930. (209 p.)

McMurtrie, D. C. "The first Texas newspaper." SHQ, XXXVI (1932), 41-46.

McMurtrie, D. C. "Pioneer printing in Texas." SHQ, XXXV (1932), 173-193.

Manning, W. R. "Texas and the boundary issue, 1822-1829." SHQ, XVII (1914), 217-261.

Marshall, T. M. "Commercial aspects of the Texan Santa Fé expedition." SHQ, XX (1917), 242-250

Marshall, T. M. "St. Vrain's expedition to the Gila in 1826." SHQ, XIX (1916), 251-260.

Marshall, T. M. "The southwestern boundary of Texas." SHQ, XIV (1911), 277-293.

Marshall, T. M. "The whereabouts of Sam Houston in 1834." SHQ, XVI (1913), 328-329.

Martin, M. E. (ed.). "From Texas to California in 1849: diary of C. C. Cox." SHQ, XXIX (1925), 36-50, 128-146, 201-223.

Martínez Caro, R. Verdadera idea de la primera campaña de Tejas y sucesos ocurridos después de la acción de San Jacinto. Mexico, 1837. (162 p.)
A volume, now very scarce, published in Mexico a year after the fall of the Alamo.

Mecham, J. L. "Antonio de Espejo and his journey to New Mexico." SHQ, XXX (1926), 114-138.

Mecham, J. L. (ed.). "Supplementary documents relating to the Chamuscado-Rodríguez expedition." SHQ, XXIX (1926), 224-231.

Miller, E. T. "The connection of Peñalosa with the La Salle expedition." SHQ, V (1901), 97-112; VI (1902), 67.

Molyneux, P. "Why Texas seceded from Mexico." SR, XVIII (1933), 307-328.

Moorehead, W. K. "Recent explorations in northwest Texas." AA, XXII (1921), new series, 1-11.

Muckleroy, A. "The Indian policy of the Republic of Texas." SHQ, XXV (1922), 229-260; XXVI (1923), 1-29, 184-206.

Nelson, A. B. "Campaigning in the Big Bend of the Río Grande in 1787." SHQ, XXXIX (1936), 200-227.

Nelson, A. B. "Juan de Ugalda and Picaxande Inst-tinsle, 1787-1788." SHQ, XLIII (1940), 438-464.
"Colonel Ugalde's successful effort to establish friendly relations between him [Picaxande Inst-tinsle, Lipiyán Apache chief] and the Spanish caused jurisdictional disputes later among the Spanish officials of the northern frontier" (Hanke, Handbook, 1940, p. 261).

Newell, C. History of the revolution in Texas. Austin, 1935. (215 p.)
Account "particularly of the war of 1835 and '36, together with the latest geographical, topographical and statistical accounts of the country from the most authentic sources, also an appendix" (subtitle).

Oberste, W. H. History of Refugio mission. Refugio, Tex., 1942. (411 p.)

O'Donnell, W. J. (trans.). "Documents: La Salle's occupation of Texas." M-A VIII (1936), 96-124; also Preliminary Studies of the Texas Catholic Historical Society (Austin), III (1936), No. 2. (33 p.)
New documents from the archives of Mexico and the Archivo General de Indias, Seville, Spain.

O'Rourke, T. P. The Franciscan Missions in Texas, 1690-1793. Washington, D. C.: The Catholic University of America press, 1927. (107 p.)

Parkman, F. La Salle and the discovery of the great West. Boston, 1894. (483 p.)
Chapters 23-29 (pp. 322-446) deal with his venture on the east coast of Texas.

Paxton, F. L. "England and Mexico, 1824-1825." SHQ, IX (1905), 138-141.

Palmer, M. (ed.). "Letter: The convention of March 6, 1836." SHQ, XII (1909), 247-248.

Parsons, E. C. "Notes on the Caddo." Menasha, Wis.: Memorials, American Anthropological Association, No. 57 (1941), 1-76.

Peña y Reyes, A. de la (ed.). Don Manuel Eduardo de Gorostiza y la cuestión de Texas: documentos históricos precedidos de una noticia biográfica. Mexico: Publicaciones de la Secretaría de relaciones exteriores, 1924. (206 p.)

Correspondence between Gorostiza, minister from Mexico to the United States, and the United States State Department.

Peña y Reyes, A. de la (comp.). Lord Aberdeen, Texas y California; colección de documentos precedida de una introducción . . . Mexico: Publicaciones de Secretaría de relaciones exteriores, 1925. (72 p.)

Portillo, E. L. Apuntes para la historia antiqua de Coahuila y Texas. Saltillo, 1886. (482 p.)

Prieto, A. Historia, geografía y estadística del estado de Tamaulipas. Mexico. D.F., 1873. (361 p.)

Rather, E. Z. "Recognition of the Republic of Mexico by the United States," SHQ. XIII (1909), 155-256.

Red, W. S. The Texas colonists and religion, 1821-1836. Austin, Tex., 1924. (149 p.)

"A centennial tribute to the Texas patriots who shed their blood that we might enjoy civil and religious liberty" (subtitle).

Reindorf, R. C. "The founding of missions at La Junta de los Ríos." M-A XX (1938), 107-131.

Richardson, R. N. "Framing the constitution of the Republic of Texas," SHQ, XXXI (1928), 191-220.

Ríos, E. E. Fray Margíl de Jesús, Apóstol de América. Mexico, 1941. (224 p.)

Chapters XIII and XIV cover Father Margil's career as missionary in Coahuila, Nuevo León, and Texas. A scholarly, documented study.

Riviere, W. T. "Sam Houston's retreat." SHQ, XLVI (1942), 9-14.

Roll, Santiago. Nuevo León. Apuntes históricos. 2 vols. Monterrey, 1938.

Rourke, C. Davy Crockett. New York, 1934. (276 p.)

Rourke, C. "Davy Crockett; forgotten facts and legends." SR, XIX (1934), 149-161.

Rubio Mañé, J. I. Los piratos Lafitte. Mexico, 1938. (240 p.)

Rutledge Gibson, G. Journal of a soldier under Kearny and Doniphan.

Saldivar, G. (ed.). "El primer impreso sobre la conquista y colonización de Tamaulipas." IH, I (1938), 82-87, 191-198, 329-332.

Copy of the act of 1740 authorizing the entrada of Escandón.

Sánchez, D. Un gran apóstol de las Américas Septentrional y Central, el V.P.Fr. Antonio Margíl de Jesús, franciscano. Guatemala, 1917. (249 p.)

Sánchez Navarro, C. La guerra de Texas. Mexico, 1938. (186 p.)

Scarborough, W. F. "Old Spanish missions in Texas." SR, XIII (1928), 155-177, 366-397, 491-504; XIV (1929), 87-105, 237-255.

Saxon, L. Lafitte, the pirate. New York, 1930. (307 p.)

Schmitt, E. J. "The name Alamo." SHQ, III (1899), 67-69.

Schmitt, E. J. "Sieur Louis de Saint Denis." SHQ, I (1898), 204-215.

Schmitt, E. J. "Question concerning Shea manuscript." SHQ, I (1898), 307.

Schmitt, E. J. Catalogue of Franciscan missionaries in Texas, 1528-1859. Austin, Tex., 1901.

Scott, F. J. Historical heritage of the Lower Rio Grande . . . 1747-1848. San Antonio, 1937. (246 p.)

"A historical record of Spanish exploration, subjugation and colonization of the lower Rio Grande valley and the activities of José Escandón, Count of Sierra Gorda, together with the development of towns and ranches under Spanish, Mexican and Texas sovereignties" (subtitle).

Scramuzza, V. M. "Galveston, a Spanish settlement of colonial Louisiana." LHQ, XIII (1930), 553-609.

Account of a settlement by the Spaniards to combat English ascendancy in the Mississippi valley, in 1779; abandoned a few years later.

Shelby, C. C. "St. Denis's second expedition to the Río Grande." SHQ, XXVII (1924), 190-216.

Shelby, C. C. "St. Denis's declaration concerning Texas in 1717." SHQ, XXVI (1923), 165-183.

Shelby, C. C., "Projected attacks upon the northeastern frontier of New Spain, 1719, 1721." HAHR, XIII (1933), 457-472.

Smith, R. C. "James W. Fannin, Jr., in the Texas Revolution." SHQ, XXIII (1919), 79-90, 171-202, 271-284.

Spell, L. M. "The first text book in Texas." SHQ, XXIX (1929), 289-295.

Deals with Bartholomé García's *Manual.*

Spell, L. M. "Samuel Bangs: the first printer in Texas." HAHR XI (1931), 248-258.

Steck, F. B. "Forerunners of Captain de León's expedition to Texas, 1670 - 1675." SHQ, XXXVI (1932), 1-28; also Preliminary Studies of the Texas Catholic Historical Society (Austin), II (1933), No. 3. (32 p.)

Based on hitherto unknown manuscript sources in the Library of the University of Texas.

Steen, R. W. "Analysis of the work of the General Council of Texas, 1835-1836." SHQ, XL (1937), 309-333; XLI (1938), 225-240, 324-348; XLII (1938), 28-54.

An important study on Texan affairs on the eve of the declaration of independence.

Sternberg, R. R. "The Texas schemes of Jackson and Houston, 1829-1836." SSSQ, XV (1934), 229-250.

Deals with the acquisition of Texas, attempting to show that Jackson and Houston had some secret understanding concerning the matter.

Sternberg, R. "Jackson's Neches claim, 1829 - 1836." SHQ, XXXIX (1936), 255-274.

Sternberg, R. R. "Andrew Jackson and the Erving affidavid." SHQ, XLI (1937), 142-153.

Sturmberg, R. History of San Antonio and of the early days in Texas. San Antonio, 1920. (130 p.)

Swanton, J. R. Linguistic material from the tribes of southern Texas and northeastern Mexico. Washington, D. C.: Government Printing Office, 1940. (145 p.)

Swanton, J. R. Source material on the history and ethnology of the Caddo Indians. Washington, D. C.: Government Printing Office, 1942. (332 p.)

Tiscareno, Angel de los Dolores. El colegio de Guadalupe desde su origen hasta nuestros días ó memorias de los acontecimientos contemporáneos que con el se relacionan, 4 vols. Mexico, 1902.

Torrente, Camilo. Old and new San Fernando. San Antonio, Tex., 1927.

Sotomayor, J. F. Historia del apostólico colegio de Nuestra Señora
de Guadalupe de Zacatecas
desde su fundación hasta nuestros dias, formada con excelen-
tes datos per el presbítero José
Francisco Sotomayor. 2 vols.
Mexico, 1889.
This is the second edition of Sotomayor's *Historia*, edited by Rafael
Ceniceros y Villareal. The episcopal
"licencia" for the first edition is
dated August 24, 1874. Contains
biographical sketches of Franciscans
who labored in Texas missions.

Tous, G. (trans.). "The Espinosa-
Olivares-Aguirre expedition of
1709." Preliminary Studies of
the Texas Catholic Historical
Society (Austin), I (1930), No.
3. (14 p.)

Tous, G. (trans.). "Ramón's expedition:" Espinosa's diary of
1716." Preliminary Studies of
the Texas Catholic Historical
Society (Austin), I (1930), No.
4. (24 p.)

Vaillant, A. (trans.). Lafitte le
pirate. Paris, 1936. (225 p.)
French translation of Lyle Saxon's work.

Valdes, J. C. Santa Ana y la guerra
de Tejas. Mexico, 1936.
A biography of Santa Ana, based
partly on unpublished papers of the
Santa Ana family, dealing with the
war between Mexico and Texas, its
background and aftermath.

Vilaplana, H. de. Vida portentosa
del Americano Septentrional
apóstol, el V. P. Fr. Antonio
Margíl de Jesús . . . Madrid,
1775. (335 p.)

Villiers du Terrage, M. de. L'expedition de Cavelier de la Salle
dans le golfe du Mexique
(1684 - 1687). Paris, 1931.
(229 p.)

**Villiers du Terrage, M. de and P.
Rivet.** "Les Indiens du Texas
et les expeditions francaises de
1720-1721 a la baie St. Bernard." Paris: Journal de la Societé des Americanistes de
Paris, XI (1914-1919). (403
ff.)

Warren, H. G. "Southern filibusters
in the war of 1812." LHQ,
XXV (1942), 291-300.

Warren, H. G. (ed.). "Documents
relating to the establishment of
privateers at Galveston, 1816-
1817." LHQ, XXI (1938),
1086-1109.

Warren, H. G. (ed.). "Documents
relating to George Graham's
proposals to Jean Lafitte for the
occupation of the Texas coast."
LHQ, XXI (1938), 213-219.

Warren, H. G. "José Álvarez de
Toledo's initiation as a filibuster,
1811 - 1813." HAHR, XX
(1940), 56-82.

Warren, H. G. "José Álvarez de
Toledo's reconciliation with
Spain and projects for suppres-
sing rebellion in the Spanish
colonies." LHQ, XXIII (1940),
827-863.

Warren, H. G. "Origin of General
Mina's invasion of Mexico."
SHQ, XLII (1938), 1-20.

West, E. H. (trans.). "Bonilla's
brief compendium of the history of Texas, 1722." SHQ,
VIII (1904), 3-78.

West, E. H. (trans.). "De León's
expedition of 1689." SHQ,
VIII (1905), 199-224.

Wharton, C. R. Republic of Texas.
Houston, 1922. (225 p.)
Covers the period from first
United States colonies in 1821 to
the annexation in 1846.

Wharton, C. R. History of Texas.
Dallas, Tex., 1935. (476 p.)

Wharton, C. R. Remember Goliad.
Houston, 1931. (61 p.)

Wharton, C. R. San Jacinto, the
sixteenth decisive battle. Houston, Tex., 1930. (138 p.)

Wharton, C. R. El presidente: a
sketch of the life of Santa Ana.
Austin, Tex., 1926. (197 p.)

Williams, A. "A critical study of the siege of the Alamo and of the personnel of its defenders." SHQ, XXXVI (1933), 251-287; XXXVII (1934), 1-44, 79-115, 157-184, 237-312.

Winston, J. E. "Kentucky and the independence of Texas." SHQ, XVI (1912), 27-62.

Winston, J. E. "Mississippi and the independence of Texas." SHQ, XXI (1917), 36-60.

Winston, J. E. "New Orleans newspapers and the Texas question, 1835-1837." SHQ, XXXVI (1932), 109-129.

Winston, J. E. "New York and the independence of Texas." SHQ, XVIII (1915), 368-385.

Winston, J. E. "The annexation of Texas and the Mississippi democrats." SHQ, XXV (1921), 1-25.

Winston, J. E. "Pennsylvania and the independence of Texas." SHQ, XVII (1914), 262-282.

Winston, J. E. "Virginia and the independence of Texas." SHQ, XVI (1913), 277-283.

Winston, J. E. "Stephen F. Austin, founder of Texas, 1763-1836." SHQ, IX (1906), 398-404.

Winters, J. W. "An account of the battle of San Jacinto." SHQ, VI (1903), 139-144.

Woldert, A. "The location of the Tejas Indian village (San Pedro) and the Spanish missions in Houston County, Texas." SHQ, XXXVIII (1935), 203-212.

Wortham, L. J. A history of Texas, from wilderness to commonwealth. 5 vols. Fort Worth, Tex., 1924.

Wooten, D. G. (ed.). A comprehensive history of Texas, 1685-1897. 2 vols. Dallas, Tex., 1898.

Ximénez Samaniego, J. (ed.). Relación de la vida de la Venerable Madre Sor María de Jesús, escritora desta obra: hazela Fray Joseph Ximénez Samaniego de la orden de San Francisco. Madrid, 1720. (676 p.)

The volume contains three parts: (1) the "Prologo Galeato" by the editor (pp. 1-96); (2) Maria de Agreda's autobiography (pp. 97-240); (3) *Notes* by Joseph Ximenez Samaniego and Juan Sendin Calderon. The account of the conversion of the Jumanos Indians takes up paragraph xii (pp. 131-137).

Yoakum, H. K. History of Texas from its first settlement in 1685 to its annexation to the United States in 1846. 2 vols. New York, 1856.

C. K. Adams regarded this work as "the product of earnest and conscientious research. At the time the book was written, however, the important sources of information concerning early Texas history contained in the Franciscan records had not been made accessible. Until these are opened, and the Spanish MSS. consulted, no history of Texas during the eighteenth century can be regarded as conclusive. But of the materials at hand this author has made good use. His style as a writer is careless; but the work is not without considerable merit" (*A Manual of Historical Literature,* p. 561). In 1935 the Steck Company of Austin published a facsimile reproduction of the original edition (1856).

Zavala, A. de. History and Legends of the Alamo and other missions in and around San Antonio. San Antonio, 1917. (219 p.)

A collection of some valuable detached pieces pertaining to Texas before and during the war of independence in Mexico.

67

VI. NEW MEXICO AND ARIZONA
1581-1846

Adams, E. B. and F. V. Scholes. "Books in New Mexico, 1598-1680." NMHR, XVII (1942), 226-255.

Alessio Robles, C. La región arqueológico de Casas Grandes de Chihuahua. Mexico, 1929. (46 p.)

Arnold, C. "The Mission of San Diego de Jemez." Pa, XXVIII (1930), 118-122.

Anthony, C. "Kit Carson, a Catholic." NMHR, XI (1935), 323-337.

Audet, F. J. "Les Canadiens au Nouveau Méxique." Quebec: Societé de geographie de Québec, Bulletin, XVII (1923), 139-163.

Ayer, Mrs. E. E. (trans.). The Memorial of Fray Alonso de Benavides, 1630. Chicago, priv. print., 1916. (309 p.)
A magnificent edition: photographic reproduction of the original with translation richly annotated by F. W. Hodge and C. F. Lummis.

Bailey, J. B. Diego de Vargas and the reconquest of New Mexico, 1692-1704. Albuquerque: University of New Mexico press, 1940. (290 p.)
An excellent study, based for the most part on original sources. Deserves a place beside the study of J. M. Espinosa and that of C. W. Hackett.

Baker, Ruth Laughlin. Caballeros. New York, 1931. (379 p.)
A summary narrative and colorful description of life in Spanish Santa Fé, N. M.

Baldwin, G. C. "Indian Tribes of Arizona." Ka, III (1938), 17-20, 21-24.

Bancroft, H. H. History of Arizona and New Mexico, 1530-1888. San Francisco, Calif., 1889. (829 p.)

Bandelier, A. F. "Pó-Sé." NMHR, I (1926), 335-350.

Bandelier, A. F. "Documentary history of the Rio Grande pueblos." NMHR, IV (1929), 303-335; V (1930), 38-67, 154-186, 240-263, 333-386.
A reprint of Bandelier's earlier study.

Bandelier, A. F. "Kin and Clan." NMHR, VIII (1933), 165-176; also Historical Society of New Mexico, Publications, No. 2 (1882). (8 p.)

Bandelier, A. F. Contributions to the history of the southwestern portion of the United States. Cambridge: Archaeological Institute of America, 1890. (206 p.)
The fifth study in this volume (pp. 179-206) deals with "the expedition of Pedro de Villazur, from Santa Fé, New Mexico, to the banks of the Platte River, in search of the French and the Pawnees, in the year 1720."

Bandelier, A. F. Historical introduction to Studies among the sedentary Indians of New Mexico. Boston: Papers of the Archaeological Institute of America, American series, I (1881). (33 p.)

Bandelier, A. F. A visit to the aboriginal ruins in the valley of the Rio Pecos. Boston: Papers of the Archaeological Institute of America. American series, I (1881). (100 p.)

Bandelier, A. F. Final report of investigations among the Indians of the southwestern United States, carried on mainly in the years from 1880 to 1885. 2 vols. Cambridge: Papers of the Archaelogical Institute of America. American series, III (1890), 1890 and 1892. (323 and 591 pp.)

Bandelier, A. F. An outline of the documentary history of the Zuñi tribe. [New York: Hemenway Southwestern Archaeological Expedition, after 1886.] (115 p.)

Bandelier, A. F. The gilded man (el Dorado) and other pictures of the Spanish occupancy of America. New York, 1893. (302 p.)

The second part of the volume, entitled "Cibola," (pp. 111-257) for the most part with New Mexico (the Seven Cities, Coronado, the New Mexican pueblos, and Quivira), while the last two essays are "The age of the City of Santa Fé" and "Jean L'Archeveque" (pp. 282-302).

Bandelier, A. F. Documentary history of the Rio Grande pueblos of New Mexico, Cambridge: Papers of the Archaeological Institute of America. American series, II (1910).

This study has been reprinted in the *New Mexico Historical Review.*

Bandelier, A. F. and E. L. Hewitt. Indians of the Rio Grande valley. Albuquerque, N. M., 1937. (274 p.)

Deals with Spanish exploration and the impact of Spanish civilization upon the native races as revealed in contemporary sources.

Bandelier, A. F. The delight makers. New York, 1890. (490 p.)

A story of Indian life, based on archaeological studies, of which C. F. Lummis says: "It will always be a standard—the most photographic story yet printed of the life of the prehistoric Americans" (Introduction, p. xvii).

Barth, A. W. "The Nieto inscription on el Morro." HAHR, XIV (1934), 352-354.

Bartlett, K. "Notes upon the route of Espejo and Farfán to the Mines in the sixteenth century." NMHR, XVII (1942), 21-36.

Basanoff, V. "Dictamen of Pedro Galindo Navarro, Auditor of Guerra, of Dec. 7, 1795." NMHR, VIII (1933), 183-200.

Discussion of that portion of the judge's opinion which "refers to the proportion of the property of deceased members of the army" (Griffin, *Writings,* 1933, p. 135) that should go to the military chaplains as stipends for saying Holy Mass for the deceased soldiers.

Basanoff, V. "Bienes castrenses." NMHR, VIII (1933), 273-303.

Beers, H. P. "Military protection of the Santa Fé trail to 1843." NMHR, XII (1937), 113-133.

Benavides, Alonso de. "Memorial." LofS, XIII (1900), 277-290, 345 - 358, 435 - 444; XIV (1901), 39-52, 137-148, 227-232.

This is an English translation of the *Memorial* of Fray Alonso de Benavides.

Bieber, R. P. (ed.) Adventures in the Santa Fé trade, by James Josiah Webb. Glendale, Calif., 1931. (316 p.)

Webb's *Adventures* is a sequel to Gregg's *Commerce of the prairies* (q. v.).

Binkley, W. C. "New Mexico and the Texan-Santa Fé expedition." SHQ, XXVII (1923), 85-107.

Deals with the attitude of the people of New Mexico toward the expedition which started from Texas in 1841 and with the preparations made in New Mexico to receive the expedition.

Bloom, L. B. "Early Weaving in New Mexico." NMHR, II 1927, 228-239.

Bloom, L. B. (trans.). "Barreiro's Ojeada sobre Nuevo Mexico." NMHR, III (1928), 73-97, 145-179; also reprint, Santa Fe: New Mexico Historical Society, 1928. (60 p.)

Translation of the Ojeada (1832) description with critical notes.

Bloom, L. B. "Beginnings of representative government in New Mexico." Pa, XII (1922), 74-78.

Deals with Spanish colonial times, local municipal government in operation.

Bloom, L. B. (ed.). "A glimpse of New Mexico in 1620." NMHR, III (1928), 357-389.
Document on difficulties between the spiritual and the temporal authorities under Governor Eulate.

Bloom, L. B. (trans.). "Instructions for Don Pedro de Peralta, Governor and Captain General of New Mexico in place of Don Juan de Oñate." Pa, XXVI (1928), 466-473.

Bloom, L. B. "When was Santa Fé founded?" NMHR, IV (1929), 188-195.

Bloom, L. B. (ed.). "A group of Kearny letters." NMHR, V (1930), 17-37, 216-217.

Bloom, L. B. (ed.). "The royal order of 1620 to Custodian Fray Estéban Perea." NMHR, V (1930), 288-299.

Bloom, L. B. "Santa Fé and the Far West in 1841." NMHR, V (1930), 299-314.

Bloom, L. B. (ed.). "A campaign against the Moqui pueblos under Governor Phelix Martínez, 1716." NMHR, VI (1931), 158-226.
"An annotated translation by the late Ralph E. Twitchell" (subtitle).

Bloom, L. B. (ed.). "Fray Estévan de Perea's Relación." NMHR, VIII (1933), 211-236.
Perea's report was published in Seville, Spain, in 1632. Here translated with an introduction.

Bloom, L. B. (ed.). "Aubuquerque and Galisteo (1706)." NMHR, X (1935), 48-51.
Certificates of their founding in 1706.

Bloom, L. B. "The governors of New Mexico." NMHR, X 1935), 152-157.
The list here published covers the entire period, from 1598 to 1935.

Bloom, L. B. (ed.). "A trade invoice of 1638." NMHR, X (1935), 242-248.
The invoice is "for goods shipped by Governor Rosas from Santa Fé."

Bloom, L. B. (trans.) "Oñate's exoneration." NMHR, XII (1937), 175-183.
The document, found by Bloom in the Archivo General de Indias (Seville, Spain), shows that Oñate before his death found favor with the King of Spain. Translation with other pertinent Oñate papers.

Bloom, L. B. "The Chihuahua highway." NMHR, XII (1937), 209-216.

Bloom, L. B. and L. B. Mitchell (trans. and ed.). "The chapter election in 1672." NMHR, XIII (1938), 85-119.
The original Latin text with English translation of the document drawn up by the Franciscans in New Mexico, with a discussion as to the site of Mission San Diego de los Jemez.

Bloom, L. B. "The Vargas encomienda." NMHR, XIV (1939), 366-417.
"A documented study of the *reconquistador's* grant of Indians in encomienda. That the encomienda was 'a system of forced labor' rather than the accorded right to collect tribute is not in accord with the best authority, including Silvio Zavala" (Hanke, *Handbook,* 1939, p. 232).

Bloom, L. B. "Two early pictures of Santa Fé." NMHR, IV (1929), 298-300.

Bloom, L. B. "The Silva Nieto inscription." NMHR, IX (1934), 94-97.

Bloom, L. B. "Inscription Rock." NMHR, IX (1934), 98.

Bloom, L. B. "Note on the Peñalosa map." NMHR, IX (1934), 228-229.

Bloom, L. B. "The Diego de Vargas Notes." NMHR, X (1935), 170-171.

Bloom, L. B. "Portrait of Diego de Vargas." NMHR, XI (1936), 208-209.

Bloom, L. B. "The Sanson map." NMHR, XI (1936), 210.

Bloom, L. B. "Our first press." NMHR, XII (1937), 107-110.

Bloom, L. B. "Gran Quivira." NMHR, XV (1940), 98-99.

Bloom, L. B. "New Mexico under Mexican administration, 1821-1846." OSFé, I (1913), 3-49, 131-175, 235-287, 347-368; II (1914), 3-56, 119-169, 223-277, 351-380.

Bloom, L. B. "Early bridges in New Mexico." Pa, XVIII (1925), 165-175.

Bloom, L. B. "Ledgers of a Santa Fé trader." Pa, XIV (1923), 133-136.

Bloom, L. B. "The emergence of Chaco Canyon in history." AaA, XI (1921), 29-35.

Bolton, H. E. Kino's historical memoir of Pimeria Alta. 2 vols. Cleveland, 1919.
"A contemporary account of the beginnings of California, Sonora, and Arizona, by Father Eusebio Francisco Kino, S. J., pioneer missionary explorer, cartographer, and ranchman, 1683-1711" (subtitle).

Bolton, H. E. The padre on horseback. San Francisco, 1932. (90 p.)
"A sketch of Eusebio Francisco Kino, S. J., Apostle to the Pimas" (subtitle).

Bolton, H. E. "French intrusion into New Mexico." The Pacific Ocean in history. (New York, 1917.)

Bolton, H. E. Rim of Christendom. New York, 1936. (644 p.)
"A biography of Eusebio Francisco Kino, Pacific Coast pioneer" (subtitle). Critical and exhaustive with a rich bibliography of Kino materials (pp. 597-627).

Bolton, H. E. (ed.). "Papers of Zebulon M. Pike, 1806-1807." AHR, XIII (1908), 798-827.

Bolton, H. E. "Father Escobar's relation of the Oñate expedition to California." CHR, V (1919), 19-41.

Bolton, H. E. "The Black Robes of New Spain." CHR, XXI (1935), 257-282.

Bolton, H. E. "Father Kino's lost History, its discovery and its value." New York: Bibliographical Society of America, Papers, VI (1911), 9-34.

Bolton, H. E. "Escalante in Dixie and the Arizona strip." NMHR, III (1928), 41-72.

Brayer, H. O. "Peter Hayleyn's cosmography of New Mexico." NMHR, XI (1936), 129-144.
A critical explanation of Hayleyn's geographical errors.

Brayer, H. O. Pueblo Indian land grants of the "Rio Abajo," New Mexico. Albuquerque: University of New Mexico press, 1939. (135 p.)

Bucher, M. "Mission San Xavier del Bac, Tucson, Arizona." HAHR, XVI (1936), 91-93.
Proves that the present structure of the mission "was entirely the work of the Franciscans" and the mission which Father Kino built lay "to the northeast, on the left bank of the [Santa Cruz] river" (pp. 91-92).

Burton, E. B. "The Taos rebellion." OSFé, I (1913), 176-209.

Campbell, T. J. "Eusebio Kino, 1644-1711." CHR, V (1920), 353-376.

Carleton, J. H. Diary of an excursion to the ruins of Abó, Quarra, and Gran Quivira, in New Mexico. Washington, D. C.: Smithsonian Institution, 9th Report, 1855, 296-316.

Chapman, C. E. "The Jesuits in Baja California, 1697-1768." CHR, VI (1920), 46-58.

Chavez, I. L. (trans.). "Instructions to Governor Peralta by the Viceroy." NMHR, IV (1929), 179-187.

Caywood, L. R. "The Spanish missions of northwestern New Spain—Jesuit period, 1687-1767 and Franciscan period, 1768-1836." Ka, V (1939), 5-8 and VI (1941), 13-16.

Coffey, F. A. "Some general aspects of the Gadsden treaty." NMHR, VIII (1933), 145-165.

Carroll, H. B. and J. V. Haggard (trans. and eds.). Three New Mexico Chronicles. Albuquerque, 1942. (342 p.)
A Quivira Society publication, No. XI. Contains Pino's *Exposicion* of 1812, Barreiro's *Ojc̣ la* of 1832, and Escudero's *Noticias*. An excellent translation with scholarly introduction and abundant critical annotations.

Carroll, H. B. "Some New Mexico-West Texas relationships." Abilene: Year Book, West Texas Historical Association, XIV (1938), 97-100.

Chávez, A. The defeat of the Comanches in 1716. Santa Fé: Publications, Historical Society of New Mexico, (1906). (9 p.)

Chávez, I. L. (trans.). "Instructions to Peralta by the Viceroy." NMHR, IV (1929), 178-187.
The document is dated March 30, 1609.

Cheetham, F. T. "Kit Carson, pathbreaker, patriot and humanitarian." NMHR, I (1926), 375-400.

Coan, C. F. History of New Mexico. 3 vols. Chicago, 1925. Vols. 2 and 3 contain biographies.

Connelley, W. E. (ed.). "A journal of the Santa Fé trail." MVHR, XII (1925), 72-98, 227-255.
The journal of a military expedition, by its commander, Captain Philip St. George Cook, whose U. S. Dragoons protected the caravan of traders from Ft. Leavenworth to the boundary of Mexico, 1843.

Conway, G. R. G. "Antonio de Espejo as a familiar of the Mexican inquisition, 1572-1578." NMHR, VI (1931), 1-20.

Cornish, B. Q. "The ancestry and family of Juan de Oñate." The Pacific Ocean in History (New York, 1917).

Cossio, D. A. Historia de Nuevo León. 6 vols. Monterrey, 1925-1933.

Coues, E. M. (ed.). On the trail of a Spanish pioneer: the diary and itinerary of Francisco Garcés . . . by Elliott Coues. 2 vols. New York, 1900. (608 p.)
The editor prefaces his translation with a critical biography of the Franciscan missionary and explorer, Francisco Garcés, and briefly discusses the friar's four entradas between 1768 and 1774.

Coues, E. M. (ed.). The expeditions of Zebulon Montgomery Pike. 3 vols. New York, 1895.

Cox, I. J. "Opening of the Santa Fé trail." MHR, XXV (1930), 30-66.

Culmer, F. A. "Marking the Santa Fé trail." NMHR, IX (1934), 78-94.

Curtis, F. S., Jr. "The influence of weapons on New Mexican history." NMHR, IV (1926), 324-334.

Curtis, F. S., Jr. "Spanish arms and armor in the Southwest." NMHR, II (1927), 107-134.

Davis, W. W. H. The Spanish conquest of New Mexico. Doylestown, Pa., 1869. (425 p.)
Davis was U. S. attorney in New Mexico in 1853-1855. According to H. H. Bancroft (*Arizona and New Mexico*), "Davis falls into some radical errors; notwithstanding the title of his book, he really knows very little of the 'conquest' proper, even putting its date seven years too early" (p. 23).

Davis, W. W. H. El Gringo; or New Mexico and her people. New York, 1857. (432 p.)
Chiefly a personal diary kept by the author during the two and half years he resided in New Mexico as U. S. attorney.

Davis, W. W. H. "The Pueblo Indian of New Mexico." Pa, XXVI (1929), 259-286.
An article by Davis, hitherto unpublished, was submitted to *El Palacio* by F. W. Hodge because "it sheds light on the Pueblo Indians as they were soon after the beginning of the American possession."

Defouri, J. H. Historical sketch of of the Catholic Church in New Mexico. San Francisco, 1887. (164 p.)

According to Hodge (*Memorial of Fray Alonso de Benavides*), the sketch "is unreliable as respects early history" (p. 235).

Dignuet, León. Chihuahua. Reseña geográfica y estadística. Paris. 1909. (40 p.); Mexico, 1912.

Document. Instructions for Pedro de Peralta, governor and captain general of New Mexico." Pa, XXIV (1928), 466-473.

Document. Relaciones de todas las cosas que en el Nuevo Mexico se han visto y savido, asi por mar como par tierra, desde el año de 1538 hasta el de 1626, by Girónimo de Zárate Salmerón. Mexico: Documentos para la historia de Mexico, 3ra serie, 1856.

A translation by C. F. Lummis was published in *Land of Sunshine*, XI (1898), 336-346; XII (1899); 39-48, 104-113, 180-187.

Document. "Exploration and settlement in New Mexico and in adjacent regions." Bolton, H. E.: Spanish Exploration in the Southwest, 1542-1706, 135-280.

Contains translation of the documents relating to the Rodríguez-Chamuscado expedition, the Espejo expedition, the Oñate expeditions, and the founding of the Province of New Mexico.

Document. "The justification of General Don Diego de Vargas." OSFé, II (1914), 57-65.

Document. "Memorial sobre las missiones de Sonora, 1722." Mexico, D. F.: Boletín, Archivo General de la Nación, IX (1938), 275-320.

A report of Fray Antonio de los Reyes to Viceroy Bucareli y Ursúa concerning the missions in Pimería Alta and Baja (Arizona and Northern Sonora).

Document. "Carta . . . escrita . . . año de 1778" by Silvesre Velez

de Escalante. LofS, II (1900), 247-250, 309-314.

The letter deals with the pueblo revolt of 1680 and discusses the location of Quivira. According to Lummis (LofS. II, 247), Father Escalante "condenses the account from official documents then [1778] in the archives at Santa Fé, to which he had access, being then one of the Franciscans active in New Mexico at the time."

Document. "Truthful report of the magnificent conversion which has been had in New Mexico, by Fray Estévan de Perea, O.F.M." LofS, XV (1901), 358-362, 466-469.

Document. "The last campaign of General de Vargas, 1704." OSFé, II (1914). 66-72.

Document. "New Mexico. Otherwise, the Voiage of Anthony of Espejo . . . Translated out of the Spanish copie printed first at Madreel, 1586, and afterward at Paris, in the same year. Imprinted at London for Thomas Cadman. [1587]." Boston: Massachusetts Historical Society. Photostat Reproductions, No. 50, American Series, 1921.

Reproduced from the original in the library of Henry E. Huntington.

Document. "Instrucciones del Virrey D. Bernardo de Gálvez para la defense de la provincias internas del Norte." Boletín Archivo General de la Nacion (Mexico, D.F.), VIII (1937), 491-540.

Document. "William Johnson's journal." LHQ, V (1922), 34-50.

Document. "Noticias que da Juan Candelaria vecino de esta villa de San Francisco Xavier de Albuquerque de edad de 84 años nació el año de 1692." NMHR, IV (1929), 274-297.

Spanish text and English translation of events in New Mexico communicated in 1776.

Document. "Some unpublished history. A New Mexican episode in 1748." LofS, VIII (1895), 74-78.

An account of the Indian attack on Pecos, January 27, 1748, drawn up by Fray Lorenzo Antonio Estremera. Spanish text and English translation.

Document. "Father Kino, 'The Apostle of California': his discoveries and explorations in California in a series of autograph letters, 1680-1687." London: Biblioteca Americana. Part II, Catalogue No. 432. Maggs Bros., 1922. (37 p.)

Thirty-three letters of Kino, addressed to the Duchess d'Aveiro y d'Arcos Maqueda, a descendant of the Portuguese house of Lancaster and known as "the Mother of the Missions" by reason of her generous benefactions on behalf of foreign missions.

Document. "The reconquest of New Mexico, 1692." OSFé, I (1913), 288-307, 420-435.

Extracts from the journal of De Vargas.

Document. "Interrogation of a Zia warrior, Bartolomé de Ojeda, at El Paso, on August 25th, 1689." San Marino, Calif.: Henry E. Huntington Library, Publications.

Document. "Arizona: the Jesuits in Pimeria Alta." Bolton, H. E.: Spanish Exploration in the Southwest, 1542-1706, 425-464.

Contains Kino's report and relations of the new conversions.

Donnell, F. S. "When Texas owned New Mexico to the Río Grande." NMHR, VIII (1933), 65-76.

Donnell, F. S. "When Las Vegas was the capital of New Mexico." NMHR, VIII (1933), 265-272.

Duell, P. Mission architecture as exampled in San Xavier del Bac. Tucson, Ariz., 1919. (135 p.)

Duffus, R. L. The Santa Fé trail. New York, 1930. (283 p.)

Dunn, W. E. "Spanish reaction against the French advance toward New Mexico." MVHR, II (1915), 348-362.

Ellison, S. (trans.). Confession and declaration of Juan Punsili, a Picuris Indian, before the Governor and Secretary at El Paso del Norte on the 20th August, 1683, relating to the causes, organization of the Rebellion of 1680 and condition of the people in the pueblos, their leader, their dissentions, their oppressions, and their resentment, all certified under the hand of the Governor and Secretary and the interpreters. San Marino, Calif.: Henry E. Huntington Library, MS., Doc. 50.

Engelhardt, Z. The Franciscans in Arizona. Harbor Springs, Mich., 1899. (236 p.)

Engelhardt, Z. "The Franciscans in New Mexico." FH, VI (June, 1918) to IX (January, 1922).

A series of well-documented articles in the Franciscan Herald. Chapters II, III, and IV comprise the much-discussed "Report of Fr. Marcos de Niza" which Engelhardt translated from the Pacheco y Cardenas text, since he had not "found it translated anywhere" (FR. VI, 281).

Engelhardt, Z. "El Yllustre Senor Xamnscado." SHQ, XXIX (1926), 296-300.

Espinosa, A. M. "Spanish folklore in New Mexico." NMHR, I (1926), 135-155; also reprint, Historical Society of New Mexico, Santa Fé, 1926. (21 p.)

Espinosa, A. M. "Speech mixture in New Mexico." The Pacific Ocean in history. (New York, 1917.)

Espinosa, G. (trans.). History of New Mexico by Gaspár Pérez de Villagrá, Alcalá, 1610. Los Angeles, 1933. (308 p.)

Volume IV of The Quivira Society Publications, "translated by Gilberto Espinosa" with "introduction and notes by F. W. Hodge" (title page). Heavily documented and richly illustrated—a magnificent publication.

Espinosa, J. M. "Notes on the lineage of Don Diego de Vargas." NMHR, X (1935), 112-121.

An "editorial correction," NMHR, X (1935), 170-171.

Espinosa, J. M. "The legend of Sierra Azul." NMHR, IX (1934), 113-158.

Emphasizes the part which the legend played in the reconquest of New Mexico.

Espinosa, J. M. "Governor Vargas in Colorado." NMHR, XI (1936), 179-187: also reprint, Historical Society of New Mexico, Santa Fé, 1936. (9 p.)

Espinosa, J. M. "Report authorizing Governor Vargas to reconquer New Mexico." NMHR, XIV (1939), 76-81.

Espinosa, J. M. "New light on the history of the reconquest of New Mexico." M-A, XXII (1940), 262-278.

Espinosa, J. M. "The Virgin of the reconquest of New Mexico." M-A, VII (1936), 79-87.

Relates how Vargas had images of the Blessed Virgin Mary carried in the battle of Santa Fé, 1693.

Espinosa, J. M. "The recapture of Santa Fé, New Mexico, by the Spaniards, December 29-30, 1693." HAHR, XIX (1939), 442-463.

Espinosa, J. M. (ed.). "Diary of Vargas's expedition into Colorado, 1694." CM, XVI (1939), 1-11.

Espinosa, J. M. Crusaders of the Rio Grande. Chicago: Loyola University press, 1942. (410 p.)

The work of a scholar, based on primary and secondary sources with a rich bibliography—a fascinating account of Vargas's reconquest of New Mexico after the revolt of 1680, together with Hackett's *Revolt of the Pueblo Indians* and Bailey's *Diego de Vargas,* the final word on this momentous period of New Mexican history.

Espinosa, J. M. (ed.). First expedition of Vargas into New Mexico, 1692. Albuquerque: University of New Mexico press, 1940. (319 p.)

Volume X of the Coronado Cuarto Centennial Publications, 1540-1940. Seven important documents with a scholarly historical introduction.

Espinosa, J. M. Spanish folk-tales from New Mexico. New York, 1937. (222 p.)

Contains 114 stories as related by the natives of New Mexico concerning traditions of the Spanish regime.

Ewing, R. C. "The Pima outbreak in November, 1751." NMHR, XIII (1938), 337-346.

Falconer, T. Letters and notes on the Texan-Santa Fé expedition, 1841-1842. New York, 1930. (159 p.)

Fernández del Castillo, F. and E. Böse (eds.). Las misiones de Sonora y Arizona. Mexico, D. F.: Publicaciones, Archivo General de la Nación, VIII, and Editorial "Cultura" (1913-1922). (413 p.)

Contains the *Favores Celestiales* and the *Relación diaria* of Father Eusebio Kino, dealing with his missionary work and explorations in Pimería Alta. An English translation was published by Bolton.

Fernández Duro, C. Don Diego de Peñalosa y su descubrimiento del reino de Quivira. Madrid, 1882.

Folmer, H. "Contraband trade between Louisiana and New Mexico in the eighteenth century." NMHR, XVI (1941), 249-274.

Folmer, H. "The Mallet expedition of 1739 through Nebraska, Kansas, and Colorado to Santa Fé." CM, XVI (1939), 161-173.

Fraps, C. L. "Hopiland." ArizHR, VI (1935), 3-46.

Geiger, M. The kingdom of St. Francis in Arizona. Santa Barbara, Calif., 1939. (55 p.)

Goodspeed, E. J. "Old chest found in mountain cave" [in the Sierra Ladrone Mountains]. Pa, XII (1922), 142-143.

Contains lengthy quotation from *Antiques* (Boston), article by E. J. Goodspeed. Tells of old books in chest, among them two Bibles.

Grant, B. C. One hundred years ago in old Taos. Taos, New Mexico, 1925. (31 p.)

Gregg, J. Commerce of the prairies. Philadelphia, 1844.

Contains, among three other accounts, the author's own "journal of a Santa Fé trader, during eight expeditions across the Great Western Prairies" (subtitle). Besides several early editions of the work, two later ones are available: (1) the R. G. Thwaites edition in the *Early Western Travels* series (2 vols.) and (2) a reprint by the Southwest Press (Dallas, Tex.) of the original edition in 1933 (1 vol., 438 p.).

Gunn, J. M. Schat-Chen. History, traditions, and narratives of the Queres Indians of Laguna and Acoma. Albuquerque, N. M., 1917. (222 p.)

Gusinde, M. "Ein zweites Memorial del Fray Alonso de Benavides aufgefunden." Vienna: Anthrop. Gesellschaft, Wien, Mitteil, LX, Nos. 2-3, pp. 186-190

Habig, M. "The builders of San Xavier del Bac." SHQ, XLI (1937), 154-166.

Hackett, C. W. "The revolt of the Pueblo Indians of New Mexico in 1680." SHQ, XV (1911), 93-147.

Hackett, C. W. "The causes for the failure of Otermin's attempt to reconquer New Mexico, 1681-1682." The Pacific Ocean in history. (New York, 1917.)

Hackett, C. W. "The retreat of the Spaniards from New Mexico in 1680 and the beginnings of El Paso." SHQ, XVI (1912), 137-168, 259-276.

This masterly study and the author's preceding study of the Revolt are now available in book form with exhaustive documentation in his *The Revolt of the Pueblo Indians*.

Hackett, C. W. "Otermin's attempt to reconquer New Mexico, 1681-1682." OSFé, XXX (1916), 44-84, 103-132.

Hackett, C. W. Revolt of the Pueblo Indians of New Mexico and Otermin's attempted reconquest, 1680-1682. 2 vols. Albuquerque: University of New Mexico press, 1942. CCX (262 and 430 pp.).

This is Vol. IX of the Coronado Cuarto Centennial Publications, 1540-1940. It embodies the three masterly monographs by C. W. Hackett and translations of original documents dealing with the Pueblo Revolt of 1680, by Charmion Clair Shelby. The work reveals the sound scholarship of the co-authors and with J. M. Espinosa's *Crusaders of the Rio Grande* it constitutes the best and final word on the revolt of 1680.

Hackett, C. W. "The location of the Tigua pueblos of Alameda, Puarey, and Sandia in 1680 and 1681." OSFé, II (1914), 381-391.

Hackett, C. W. "New light on Don Diego de Peñalosa: Proof that he never made an expedition from Santa Fé to Quivira and the Mississippi River in 1662." MVHR, VI (1919), 313-335.

Hackett, C. W. "Causes for the failure of Otermin's attempt to reconquer New Mexico, 1681-1692." The Pacific Ocean in History (New York, 1917).

Haley, J. E. "The Comanchero trade." SHQ, XXXVIII (1934), 157-176.

Hammond, G. P. "The conviction of Don Juan de Oñate, New Mexico's first governor." New Spain and the Anglo-American West. Los Angeles, Calif., 1932. I, 67-80.

Hammond, G. P. "Oñate and the founding of New Mexico." NMHR, I (1926), 42-78, 156-193, 292-324, 445-478; II (1927), 37-67, 134-175.

Based almost entirely on original sources with the "official list of the soldiers who accompanied Oñate to New Mexico in 1598, in alphabetical order" (pp. 187-210).

77

Hammond, G. P. Don Juan de Oñate and the founding of New Mexico. Santa Fé, N. M.: El Palacio press, 1927. (228 p.)
The six articles (listed above) published in book form by the Historical Society of New Mexico (Vol. II, October, 1927).

Hammond, G. P. and A. Rey (eds.). Expedition into New Mexico made by Antonio de Espejo, 1582-1583, as revealed in the Journal of Diego Pérez de Luxan . . . Los Angeles, 1929. (143 p.)
Vol. I of the Quivira Society publications.

Hammond, G. P. and T. C. Donnelly. The story of New Mexico, its history and government. Albuquerque: University of New Mexico press, 1936. (331 p.)

Hammond, G. P. and A. Rey. (trans. and eds.). New Mexico in 1602—Juan de Montoya's relation of the discovery of New Mexico. Albuquerque, 1938. (143 p.)
Vol. VIII of the Quivira Society Publications. An excellent translation of Montoya's Relación with a scholarly introduction (pp. 13-36) and a facsimile reproduction of the Relación.

Hammond, G. P. "The conviction of Don Juan de Oñate, New Mexico's first governor." New Spain and the Anglo-American West, Los Angeles, 1932, I 67-80.

Hammond, G. P. and A. Rey. "The Rodríguez expedition to New Mexico." NMHR, II (1927), 239-268, 334-362.

Hammond, G. P. "Pimería Alta after Kino's time." NMHR, IV (1929), 220-238.

Hammond, G. P. (trans.). "The Zúñiga journal, Tucson to Santa Fé: the opening of a Spanish trade route, 1788-1795." NMHR, VI (1931), 40-65; also reprint, Historical Society of New Mexico, Santa Fé, 1931. (26 p.)

Hammond, G. P. "Oñate a marauder?" NMHR, X (1935), 249-271.

Hammond, G. P. (ed.). "Oñate's appointment as governor of New Mexico." NMHR, XIII (1928), 241-248.

Hammond, G. P. and A. Rey. (eds.). "The Rodríguez expedition to New Mexico, 1581-1582." NMHR, II (1927), 239-268, 334-362; also reprint, New Mexico Historical Society, Santa Fé, 1927. (69 p.)
A translation of the Gallegos Relación of the Rodríguez-Chamuscado expedition.

Hammond, G. P. "The desertion of Oñate's colony from New Mexico." NDUJ, XV (1925), 154-167.

Haynes, H. W. "Early explorations of New Mexico." Narrative and Critical History of North America, II, 374-504.

Henderson, A. C. Brothers of light —the Penitentes of the Southwest. New York, 1937. (126 p.)
A descriptive account based on personal experiences; sympathetic in tone and treatment.

Hewett, E. L. Ancient life in the American Southwest. Indianapolis, Ind., 1930. (392 p.)

Hewett, E. L. "My neighbors, the Pueblo Indians." Pa, XV (1923), 123-134.

Hewett, E. L. Antiquities of the Jemez plateau, New Mexico. Washington, D. C.: Bureau of American Ethnology, Bulletin, No. 32, 1906.

Hill, J. J. "The old Spanish trail: a study of Spanish and Mexican trade from New Mexico to the Great Basin and California." HAHR, IV (1921), 444-473.
From the Rivera expedition in 1765 to that of León in 1851.

Hill, J. J. "New light on Pattie and the southwestern fur trade." SHQ, XXVI (1923), 243-254.
An account of an expedition down the Gila and up the Colorado, 1826-1827.

Hodge, F. W. History of Hawikuh, New Mexico, one of the so-called Seven Cities of Cíbola. Los Angeles, 1937. (155 p.)
An authoritative study of the expeditions and reports connected with the pueblo.

Hodge, F. W. "Recent excavations at Hawikuh." Pa, XII (1922), 2-11.
An interesting study with historical data.

Hodge, F. W. "The six cities of Cíbola." NMHR, I (1926), 478-488; also reprint, Historical Society of New Mexico, Santa Fé, 1926. (12 p.)

Hodge F. W. Bibliography of Fray Alonso de Benavides. New York: Museum of the American Indian, Heye Foundation, Indian Notes and Monographs, 1919. (39 p.)
This is a reprint of Note 2 in Ayer's translation of the Memorial of Father Benavides.

Hodge F. W. "A Virginian in New Mexico, 1773-1774." NMHR, IV (1929), 239-274.

Hodge, F. W. "French intrusion toward New Mexico in 1695." NMHR, IV (1929), 72-77.

Hodge, F. W. The age of the Zuñi pueblo of Kechipauan. New York: Museum of the American Indian, Heye Foundation, Indian Notes and Monographs, 1920. (60 p.)

Hodge, F. W. "Biographical sketch and bibliography of Adolph Francis Bandelier." NMHR, VII (1932), 353-370; also reprint of the Historical Society of New Mexico, Santa Fé, 1932. (18 p.)

Hodge, F. W. "Combs' narrative of the Santa Fé expedition in 1841." NMHR, V (1930), 305-315.

Hodge, F. W. "Pueblo names in the Oñate documents." NMHR, X (1935), 36-48.

Hodge, F. W. "The Jumano Indians." Proceedings, American Antiquarian Society, XX (1910), 249-268.

Holweck, F. G. "Note on Kino's name and nationality." CHR, VI (1921), 378-380.

Hooton, E. A. The Indians of Pecos Pueblo. New Haven: Yale University press, 1930. (391 p.)

Horgan, P. Habit of empire. Santa Fé, 1939 and New York, 1941. (114 p.)
The story of Juan de Oñate's conquest and Zaldivar's storming of the stronghold of the Acoma Indians.

Horgan, P. "The lost journals of a southwestern frontiersman." SHQ, XLIV (1940), 1-15.

Hughes, J. T. Doniphans's expedition and conquest of New Mexico and California. Washington, D. C.: Government Printing Office, 1914. (144 p.)

Hulbert, A. B. (ed.). Southwest on the turquoise trail; the first diaries on the road to Santa Fé. Denver, Colorado, 1933. 301 p.

Hull, D. "Castaño de Sosa's expedition to New Mexico in 1590." OSFé, III (1916), 307-331.

Ives, R. L. "Melchior Díaz—the forgotten explorer." HAHR, XVI (1936), 86-90.
Attempt to trace the route followed by Díaz. See HAHR, XVII (1937), pp. 146-148, for a "communication" to the editor by Carl Sauer and a reply by Ives concerning the matter.

Ives, R. L. (trans. and ed.). "The report of the bishop of Durango on conditions in northwestern Mexico in 1745." HAHR, XIX (1939), 314-317.
A brief picture of conditions on the eve of the Indian uprising of 1750.

James, G. W. Arizona, the wonderland. Boston, 1917. (478 p.)

James, G. W. The wonders of the Colorado desert. 2 vols. Boston, 1906.

James, G. W. New Mexico, the land of the delightmakers. Boston, 1920. (469 p.)

James, G. W. The Grand Canyon of Arizona. Boston, 1910. (265 p.)

James, G. W. In and around the Grand Canyon. Boston, 1913. (341 p.)

James, G. W. Indians of the painted desert region. Boston, 1903. (260 p.)

James, G. W. The Indians of the Painted Desert Region: Hopis, Navahoes, Wallapais, Havasupais. Boston, 1904. (268 p.)

Johnson, H. P. "Diego Martínez de Hurdaide: defender of the northwestern frontier of New Spain." PHR, XI (1942), 169-185.

Jones, H. "Uses of wood by the Spanish colonists in New Mexico." VII (1932), 273-291; IX (1934), 244, 245.

Kearny, T. "Kearny and 'Kit' Carson as interpreted by Stanley Vestal." NMHR, V (1930), 1-16.

Keech, R. A. "The Saline Pueblo Strongholds." Pa, XXXIV (1933), 1-13.

Keech, R. A. "To Chaco Canyon." Pa, XXXV (1933), 161-181.
   An interesting and informative description of a trip to the canyon by way of Laguna, the Enchanted Mesa, and Acoma.

Keleher, W. A. "Law of the New Mexico land grant." NMHR, IV (1929), 350-371.

Kelly, H. W. Franciscan missions of New Mexico, 1740-1760. Albuquerque: University of New Mexico press, 1941. (94 p.)

Kelly, H. W. "Franciscan missions of New Mexico, 1740-1760." NMHR, XV (1940), 345-368; XVI (1941); also reprint Historical Society of New Mexico, Santa Fé, X (1941). (94 p.)
   The study is based on primary and secondary sources.

Kelly, J. C. "The route of Antonio de Espejo down the Pecos River and across the Trans-Pecos region in 1583: its relation to West Texas archaeology." Alpine, Tex.: West Texas Historical and Scientific Society, Publications, No. 7 (1937), 7-25.

Kendall, G. W. Narrative of the Texan Santa Fé expedition comprising a description of a tour through Texas and across the great southwestern prairies . . . to the city of Mexico. 2 vols. Austin, Tex., 1935.
   "A facsimile reproduction of the original," including title-page of the two-volume London edition of 1844. An edition (585 p.) appeared in Chicago in 1929. It contains Vol. I and the first chapter of Vol. II of the 1844 Philadelphia edition.

Keyes, C. "Quest of the Gran Quivira." AHR, VI (1935), 47-58.
   Discusses Coronado's expedition into Arizona in search of the treasure called "La Gran Quivira."

Kidder, A. V. An introduction to the study of southwestern archaeology with a preliminary account of the excavations at Pecos. New Haven: Yale University press, 1924. (151 p.)

Kidder, A. V. The artifacts of Pecos. New Haven: Yale University press, 1932. (314 p.)

Kubler, G. "Gran Quivira-Humanas." NMHR, XIV (1939), 418-421.
   Identifies Gran Quivira mission with the Jumanos pueblo.

Kubler, G. (trans. and ed.). The rebuilding of San Miguel at Santa Fé in 1710. Colorado Springs, Colorado: Taylor Museum, 1939. (27 p.)

Reproduction and translation of original Spanish document concerning restoration work carried on in 1709-1710 on the old mission partially destroyed during the Pueblo revolt of 1680.

Kubler, G. The religious architecture of New Mexico in the colonial period and since the American occupation. Colorado Springs, Colorado: Taylor Museum, 1940. (232 p.)

A valuable contribution, well documented and richly illustrated.

Laumbach, V. "Las Vegas before 1850." NMHR, VIII (1933), 241-265.

Lee, L. F. "Los Hermanos Penitentes." Pa, VIII (1920), 3-20.

A study of the Penitentes observances with an English translation of ritual hymns.

Leonard, I. A. (trans. and ed.). The Mercurio Volante of Don Carlos de Sigüenza y Góngora. Los Angeles, 1932. (136 p.)

This is Vol. III of the Quivira Society Publications—a critical translation with facsimile reproduction of the original which is "an account of the first expedition of Don Diego de Vargas into New Mexico in 1692."

Lockwood, F. C. Story of the Spanish missions of the middle Southwest. Santa Ana, Calif., 1934. (78 p.)

This is "a complete survey of the missions founded by Padre Eusebio Kino in the seventeenth century and later enlarged and beautified by the Franciscan fathers during the last part of the eighteenth century" (subtitle).

Lockwood, F. C. The Apache Indians. New York, 1938. (348 p.)

Lockwood, F. C. With Padre Kino on the trail. Tucson, Arizona: University of Arizona press, 1934. (142 p.)

López de Zárate Vargas y Pimentel, D. Breve descripción genealógica de la ilustre cuanto antiquísima casa de los Vargas de Madrid. Madrid, 1740.

Loyola, Sister M. "The American occupation of New Mexico." NMHR, XIV (1939), 34-75, 143-199, 230-286.

Lummis, C. F. The land of poco tiempo. New York, 1921. (310 p.)

Lummis, C. F. The enchanted burro. Chicago, 1912. (277 p.)

Lummis, C. F. (trans. and ed.). "Testimonio on the first Comanche raid, 1748." LofS, VIII (1898), 160-165.

Lummis, C. F. "An American passion play—the Penitentes of New Mexico." LofS, IV (1894), 255-265.

Lummis, C. F. "A New Mexican episode in 1748." LofS, VIII (1898), 74-78, 126-130.

Lummis, C. F. "Opinion of Governor Codallos y Tabal." LofS, 1898.

Lummis, C. F. The Spanish pioneers. Chicago, 1893. (292 p.)

A fascinating book on the pioneers by a pioneer, most of the second part dealing with the Spanish Southwest. A number of editions since 1893.

Lummis, C. F. Mesa, Canyon, and Pueblo. New York, 1925. (517 p.)

Maas, O. (ed.). Misiones de Nuevo Mexico. Documentos del Archivo general de Indias (Sevilla) publicados por primera vez y anotados. Madrid, 1929. (272 p.)

In handy book form, the original documents previously published in AIA. The Prologo (v-lvi) has the Index of the MS, in the Biblioteca Nacional de Madrid, of *Historia de la Conquista, Perdida, y Restauración de el Reyno y Provincias de la [Nuevo] Mexico en la América Septentrional*, by Juan de Villagutierre y Sotomayar (x-lvi).

Maas, O. "Documentos sobre las misiones de Sinaloa y Nuevo Mexico." AIA, XIX (1923), 41-74.

Maas, O. "Documentos sobre las misiones de Nuevo Mexico." AIA, XX (1923), 195-209; XXI (1924), 96-113, 369-384; XXXII (1929), 76-108, 226-250, 365-385; XXXIII (1930), 81-111, 251-270, 374-395.
A collection of documents from the Archivo General de Indias, Seville. Published also in book form.

Maas, O. (ed.). Viajes de misioneros franciscanos a la conquista del nuevo mundo. Sevilla, 1915. (208 p.)
Publication of eight original documents from the Archivo General de Indias (Sevilla), all of which deal with our Spanish Southwest, notably diaries of Fathers Olivares and Espinosa in Texas, Father Escalante in northwestern New Mexico, and Father Garcés in Arizona.

Maas, O. (ed.). Las órdenes religosas de España y la colonización de América en la segunda parte del siglo XVIII. 2 vols. Barcelona, 1918 and 1929. (216 and 217 pp.)
A series of 36 lengthy documents from the Archivo General de Indias (Sevilla), two of which, in the second volume, deal specifically with New Mexico.

Maas, O. "Die ersten Versuche einer Missionierung und Kolonisierung Neumexikos." IAA, VI (1933), 345-378.

MacHarg, J. B. "The lions of Cochití." Pa, XX (1926), 99-104.
A "tentative bibliography for the study of the lions of Cochití."

Marshall, T. M. "St. Vrain's expedition to the Gila in 1826." The Pacific Ocean in history (New York, 1917).

McClintock, J. H. Arizona, the youngest state. 3 vols. Phoenix, Arizona, priv. print., 1939.

McMurtrie, D. C. "The history of early printing in New Mexico, with bibliography of known issues, 1934-1860." NMHR, IV (1929), 372-410.

McMurtrie, D. C. Memorias sobre la vida del presbítero Don Antonio José Martínez. Santa Fé, 1903.

Mange, J. M. Luz de tierra incognita enla America Septentrional y diario de las exploraciones en Sonora. Mexico, D.F.: Publicaciones, Archivo General de la Nación, X (1926).

Mecham, J. L. "The martyrdom of Father Juan de Santa Maria." CHR, VI (1921), 308-321.
A reply to this article by Zephyrin Engelhardt, defending Juan de Santa Maria, appeared in The Southwestern Catholic (San Antonio, Texas) for January 6th and 13th, 1922.

Mecham, J. L. "The second Spanish expedition to New Mexico." NMHR, I (1926), 265-291, 371, 478; II (1927), 103.
Deals with the Chamuscado-Rodríguez expedition.

Mecham, J. L. "Antonio de Espejo and his journey to New Mexico." SHQ, XXX (1926), 114-138.

Mecham, J. L. "Supplementary documents relating to the Chamuscado-Rodríguez expedition." SHQ, XXIX (1926), 224-231.

Mecham, J. L. "Francisco de Urdiñola, governor of Nueva Vuzcaya." Los Angeles, Calif.: New Spain and the Anglo-American West, Los Angeles, 1932, I. 39-65.

Meyer, T. St. Francis and the Franciscans in New Mexico. Santa Fé, N. M.: Historical Society of New Mexico, Publications (1926). (40 p.)

Mills, H. E. "Father Jacobo Sedelmayer, S.J.: a forgotten chapter in Arizona missionary history." ArizHR; VII (1936), 3-18.

Mindeleff, V. A study of pueblo architecture: Tusayan and Cíbola. Washington, D. C.: Bureau of Ethnology, 8th Report, 1891.

Morfi, J. A. Viaje de indios y diario de Nueva Mexico. Documentos para la historia de Mexico, 3ra serie, I, 307-487.
An edition was published in Mexico D. F. (Antigua Libreria Robredo de José Porría y Hijos) in 1935.

Morley, S. G. Santa Fé architecture. OSFé, II (1915), 278-301.

Mota Padilla, M. de la. Conquista del reino de la Nueva-Galicia en la América Septentrional Año de 1742. Mexico, D.F.; Boletín, Sociedad Mexicana de Geográfia y Estadística, 1870. (523 p.)

Murphy, R. "The journey of Pedro de Rivera, 1724-1728." SHQ, XLI (1937), 125-141.

N. N. The stone idols of New Mexico. Santa Fe: Publications, Historical Society of New Mexico, No. 3, 1896. (17 p.)

N. N. "Was Father Francis Eusebio Kino an Italian?" CHR, VIII (1922), 275-277.

N. N. "The martyrs of the Colorado, 1781, and the identification of the place where they died." USCHM (1887), 319-328.
Deals with the Franciscan missionaries, Francisco Garcés and companions.

N. N. "Catalogue of books in the Library of the Society relating tó New Mexico and the Southwest. Santa Fé: Publications, Historical Society of New Mexico, No. 15, 1910. (49 p.)

Ocaranza, F. Establecimientos franciscanos en el misterioso reino de Nuevo Mexico. Mexico, D.F., 1934. (202 p.)

Ocaranza, F. Crónica de las provincias internas de Nueva España. Mexico, D.F., 1939. (356 p.)

Ocaranza, F. Parva crónica de la Sierra Madre y las Pimerías Mexico, 1942. (156 p.)
Selections from original sources dealing with the northwest frontier of Mexico during the seventeenth and eighteenth centuries.

O'Gorman, J. J. "The Franciscans in New Mexico in the sixteenth century." ER, LXXXI (1929), 244-270.

O'Hara, J. F. "Benavides memorials." CHR, III (1917), 76-78.

O'Rourke, T. P. "A study of the 'Memorial' of Fray Alonso de Benavides." RACHSP, XXXIX (1928), 239-259.

Parsons, E. C. Pueblo-Indian religion. 2 vols. Chicago: Chicago University press, 1939. (1275 p.)
An interesting and important synthetic treatment.

Parsons, E. C. Taos tales. New York, 1940. 185 p.)

Pérez Balsera, J. Laudemus viros gloriosos et parentes nostros in generatione sua. Madrid, 1931.

Pérez, L. "Relación de la expedición que en 1601 hizo Juan de Oñate en el Nuevo Mexico." AIA, V (1916), 242-263.

Perrine, F. S. "Military escorts on the Santa Fé trail." NMHR, II (1927), 175-193, 269-304.

Pettis, G. H. Carson's fight with the Comanches at Adobe Walls. Santa Fé: Publications, Historical Society of New Mexico, No. 12, 1908. (35 p.)

Ponce de León, J. M. Datos geográficos y estadísticos del estado de Chihuahua. Chihuahua, 1907.

Portillo y Weber, J. L. La conquista de la Nueva Galicia. Mexico, D. F., 1935. (279 p.)

Prince, L. B. and D. T. Lawton. Addresses delivered at the dedi' cation of the Cross of Martyrs (Pueblo Revolt), September 15, 1920. Santa Fé, N. M., 1920. (23 p.)
With an introduction by R. E. Twitchell.

Prince, L. B. A concise history of New Mexico. Cedar Rapids, Iowa, 1912; 2nd edition, 1914. (272 p.)

Prince, L. B. (ed.). The Franciscan Martyrs of 1680. Santa Fé: His' torical Society of New Mexico, Publications, No. 7, 1906. (28 p.)
Translation of the "Funeral ora-tion over the twenty-one Franciscan missionaries killed by the Pueblo In-dians, August 10, 1680, preached by Doctor Ysidro Sariñana y Cuenca, March 20, 1681" (subtitle).

Prince, L. B. The Spanish mission churches in New Mexico. Cedar Rapids, Iowa, 1915. (373 p.)

Prince, L. B. Historical sketches of New Mexico. New York and Kansas City, 1883. (327 p.)

Prince, L. B. The stone lions of Cochití. Santa Fé: Publications, Historical Society of New Mex' ico, No. 4, 1903.

Ramírez Cabañas, J. (ed.). Descrip' ción geográfica de los reinos de Nueva Galicia, Nueva Vizcaya, y Nuevo León. Mexico, 1930; 2nd edition, 1940. (238 p.)
A description of the diocese of Guadalajara, written about 1605, by Alonso de la Mota y Escobar, with biographical and critical notes by the editor.

Ramona, Sister M. "The ecclesiasti' cal status of New Mexico, 1680' 1875." CHR, XIV (1929), 525-568.

Ramos Arizpe, M. Memoria sobre el estado de las Provincias In' ternas de Oriente presentada a las Cortes de Cádiz. Cadiz, 1912; Guadalajara, 1813; Phila' delphia, 1814; Mexico, D. F., 1932. (137 p.)

Rapp, I. H. "Los Pastores is gem of miracle plays." Pa, XI (1921), 151-163.
Prints, in English, the text of the play, as presented in the Christmas season in New Mexico.

Read, B. M. Illustrated- history of New Mexico. Santa Fé, 1912. (812 p.)

Read, B. M. A treatise on the dis' puted points in the history of New Mexico. Santa Fé, N. M., priv. print., 1919. (18 p.)

Read, B. M. "In Santa Fé during the Mexican régime." NMHR, II (1927), 90-98.

Read, B. M. "Perils of the Santa Fé trail in its early days, 1822' 1852." Pa, XIX (1925), 206' 211.

Read, B. M. "El Santuario de Chi' mayo." Pa, III (1916), 81-84.

Reagan, A. B. The Jemez Indians. Pa, IV (1917), 25-72.

Reuter, B. A. "Restoration of Acoma Mission." Pa, XXII (1927), 79-87.

Rippy, J. F. "A ray of light on the Gadsden treaty." SHQ, XXIV (1921), 235-242.

Rippy, J. F. "The boundary of New Mexico and the Gadsden treaty." HAHR, IV (1921) 716-742.

Rippy, J. F. "Anglo-American fili' busters and the Gadsden treaty." HAHR, V (1922), 155-180.

Rippy, J. F. "The negotiation of the Gadsden treaty." SHQ, XXVII (1923), 1-26.

Rister, C. C. Border captives. Nor' man: University of Oklahoma press, 1940. (220 p.)

Roediger, V. M. Ceremonial cos' tumes of the Pueblo Indians; their evolution, fabrication, and significance in the prayer drama. Berkeley: University of Califor' nia press, 1941. (251 p.)

Romero, C. (ed.). "Apología" of presbyter Antonio J. Martínez. NMHR, III (1928), 325-346.

The *apología* is a "statement of merits of the presbyter Antonio José Martínez, resident of the bishopric of Durango, acting pastor of Taos, in the department of New Mexico, 1838" (subtitle).

Romero, C. "A unique American chronicle." Pa, XXIV (1928), 154-165.

Discusses the significance of the Spanish language as it is spoken in New Mexico.

Ross, E. C. "The Quivira village." Topeka: Kansas State Historical Society, Collections, XVII (1928), 514-534.

Rowland, D. (ed.). "A project for exploration presented by Juan Bautista de Anza." ArizHR, VII (1936), 10-18.

Rowland, D. "The Sonora frontier of New Spain." New Spain and the Anglo-American West. Los Angeles, Calif., 1932. I, 147-164.

Rush, E. M. "Indian legends: tales of the Hopi." Pa, XXXII (1932), 137-154.

Salpointe, J. B. Soldiers of the cross. Notes on the ecclesiastical history of New Mexico, Arizona and Colorado. Banning, Calif., 1898. (299 p.)

Still valuable, based on what were then the best sources and written by the former archbishop of Santa Fé. Copies of the rare volume are still available at the place of publication, St. Boniface Industrial School, Banning, California.

Saravia, A. G. Apuntes para la historia de la Nueva Vizcaya. No. I, La Conquista. Tacubaya, Mexico, 1939. (295 p.)

Sauer, C. O. The road to Cíbola. Berkeley: University of California press, 1932. (58 p.)

Sauer, C. O. The distribution of aboriginal tribes and languages in northwestern Mexico. Berkeley: University of California press, 1934. (94 p.)

Sauer, C. O. (ed.). "A Spanish expedition into Arizona Apacheria." ArizHR, VI (1935), 3-13.

Translation of a journal of a Spanish expedition, made about 1793, into Arizona.

Scholes, F. V. "Manuscripts for the history of New Mexico in the National Library in Mexico City." NMHR, III (1928); 301-323; also reprint, Historical Society of New Mexico, Santa Fé, 1928. (23 p.)

Scholes, F. V. "Documents for the history of the New Mexican missions in the seventeenth century." IV (1929), 45-58, 195-201.

Scholes, F. V. "The supply service of the New Mexican missions in the seventeenth century." NMHR, V (1930), 93-115, 186-210, 386-404.

Scholes, F. V. "Problems in the early ecclesiastical history of New Mexico." NMHR, VII (1932), 32-74; also reprint, Historical Society of New Mexico, Santa Fé, 1932. (43 p.)

Scholes, F. V. "Civil government and society in New Mexico in the seventeenth century." NMHR, (1935), 71-111; also reprint, Historical Society of New Mexico, Santa Fe, 1935. (41 p.)

Scholes, F. V. "The first decade of the Inquisition in New Mexico." NMHR, X (1935), 195-241; also reprint, Historical Society of New Mexico, Santa Fé, 1935. (47 p.)

Scholes, F. V. "Church and state in New Mexico, 1610-1650." NMHR, XI (1936), 9-76, 145-178, 283-294, 297-349; XII (1937), 78-106; also reprint, Historical Society of New Mexico, Santa Fé, 1937. (206 p.)

Scholes, F. V. "Troublous times in New Mexico, 1659 - 1670." NMHR, XII (1937), 134-174, and volumes following, to date.

Scholes, F. V. "Notes on Sandia and Puaray." Pa, XLII (1937), 57-59.

Scholes, F. V. "Notes on the Jemez missions in the seventeenth century." Pa, XLIV (1938), 61-71, 93-102.

Scholes, F. V. and H. P. Mera. "Some aspects of the Jumano Problem." Washington, D. C.: Carnegie Institution of Washington, Publication 523 (1940), 265-299.

Sedgwick, M. K. (Rice.). (ed.). Acoma, the sky city; a study in Pueblo-Indian history and civilization, by Mrs. William T. Sedgwick. Cambridge: Harvard University press, 1927. (314 p.)

Sena, J. D. "Archives in the office of the Cadastral Engineer at Santa Fé." Pa, XXXVI (1934), 113-121.
A report on old Spanish documents in the post office building at Santa Fé.

Sena, J. D. "The chapel of Don Antonio José Ortíz." NMHR, XIII (1938), 347-359; XV (1940), 170, 182, 183.

Shea, J. G. The expedition of Don Diego Dionisio de Peñalosa from Santa Fé to the River Meschipi and Quivira in 1662, as described by Father Nicholas de Freytas; with an account of Peñalosa's projects to aid the French to conquer the mining country in Northern Mexico; and his connection with Cavelier de la Salle. New York, 1882. (101 p.)

Shine, M. A. "In favor of the Loup site." NH, VII (1924), 83-87.
Attempt to determine where the Villasur expedition met disaster and death in 1720.

Simpson, L. B. (ed.). "Commission of Francisco de Ibarra for the conquest of Nueva Vizcaya." HAHR, XIV (1934), 65-70.

Spell, L. M. "Music teaching in New Mexico in the seventeenth century." NMHR, II (1927), 27-36; also reprint, Historical Society of New Mexico, Santa Fé, 1927. (12 p.)

Steck, F. B. "Fray Nicolás de Freitas rehabilitado." DH, II (1940), 595-596.
The friar who sided with Governor Diego de Peñalosa of New Mexico, again in good standing.

Stitz, P. "Kalifornische briefe des P. Eusebio Francisco Kino (Chini) nach der overdeutschen Provinz, 1683-1685." AHSJ, III (1934), 108-128.

Stoner, V. R. "The Spanish missions of the Santa Cruz Valley." Ka, I (1936), No. 9. (4 p.)

Stoner, V. R. "Original sites of the Spanish missions of the Santa Cruz Valley." Ka, II (1937), 25-32; also in SHQ, XLI (1937), 154-163.

Thomas, A. B. "Documents bearing upon the northern frontier of New Mexico, 1818-1819." NMHR, IV (1929), 146-164; also reprint, Historical Society of New Mexico, Santa Fé, 1929.

Thomas, A. B. (ed.). "Governor Mendinueta's proposals for the defense of New Mexico, 1772-1778." NHMR, VI (1931), 21-39.

Thomas, A. B. (ed.). "An anonymous description of New Mexico, 1818." SHQ, XXXIII (1929), 50-74.

Thomas, A. B. "An eighteenth century Comanche document." AA, XXXI (1929), 289-298.
Deals with a Comanche pro-Spanish campaign in 1786 against the Apaches.

Thomas, A. B. "The massacre of the Villasur expedition, at the forks of the Platte River, August 12, 1720." NH, VII (1924), 68-81.

Thomas, A. B. "San Carlos: A Comanche pueblo on the Arkansas River, 1787." CM, VI (1929), 79-91.

Thomas, A. B. "Spanish expeditions into Colorado." CM, I (1924), 289-300.
Expeditions during the 17th and 18th centuries.

Thomas, A. B. "Spanish exploration of Oklahoma, 1599-1792." CO, VI (1928), 186-213.

Thomas, A. B. "The first Santa Fé expedition, 1792-1793." CO, IX (1931), 195-208.

Thomas, A. B. (trans. and ed.). Teodoro de Croix and the northern frontier of New Spain, 1776-1783. Norman: University of Oklahoma press, 1941. (273 p.)
Translation of documents with a splendid historical introduction (3-68) and a rich bibliography (247-268).

Thomas, A. B. "Antonio de Bonilla and Spanish plans for the defense of New Mexico, 1772-1778." New Spain and the Anglo-American West, Los Angeles, 1932. I, 183-210.

Thomas, A. B. (trans. and ed.). Forgotten frontiers. A study of the Spanish Indian policy of Don Juan Bautista de Anza, Governor of New Mexico, 1777-1787. Norman: University of Oklahoma press, 1932. (420 p.)
Translation of seventy-three valuable documents, preceded by an excellent study (pp. 1-84) of New Mexican affairs during Anza's régime. Contains (pp. 87-114) among the documents Father Morfi's *Descripcion geográfica del Nuevo Mexico . . . Año* 1782.

Thomas, A. B. (trans. and ed.). After Coronado—Spanish exploration northeast of New Mexico, 1696-1727. Norman: University of Oklahoma press, 1935. (307 p.)
Translation of nine groups of documents with a historical introduction (pp. 1-49), well written and copiously documented.

Thomas, A. B. The Plains Indians and New Mexico, 1751-1778: A collection of documents illustrative of the history of the eastern frontier of New Mexico. Albuquerque: University of New Mexico press, 1940. (232 p.)
This is Vol. XI of the Coronado Cuarto-Centennial Publications, 1540-1940. Six groups of valuable documents in English dress, with a historical introduction (pp. 1-59), dealing with eastern New Mexico from 1600 to 1778.

Thorpe, J. R. The town of Santa Fé, New Mexico (A.D. 1604); the Bishop's Lodge, Santa Fé. Santa Fé, 1921. (77 p.)

Toulouse, J. H., Jr. The mission of San Gregorio de Abó. Pa, XLV (1938), 103-107.

Treutlein, T. E. "Father Pfefferkorn and his description of Sonora." M-A, XX (1938), 229-252.
Ignacio Pfefferkorn was active as missionary in the Jesuit missions of northern Sonora after the middle of the eighteenth century.

Twitchell, R. E. Dr. Josiah Gregg, historian of the Santa Fé trail. Santa Fé; Publications, Historical Society of New Mexico, No. 26, 1924. (45 p.)

Twitchell, R. E. (trans.). Old Santa Fé: the story of New Mexico's ancient capital. Santa Fé, N. M., 1925. (488 p.)
Translation of documents from the General Land Office in Santa Fé.

Twitchell, R. E. "Pueblo Indian land tenures in New Mexico and Arizona." Pa, XII (1922), 31-33, 38-61.

Twitchell, R. E. "Captain Don Gaspár de Villagrá, author of the first history of the conquest of New Mexico by the adelantado Don Juan de Oñate." Pa, XVII (1924), 208-217; also reprint, Historical Society of New Mexico, Publications, 1924, No. 28, (11 p.)

87

Twitchell, R. E. History of the military occupation of New Mexico, 1846-1851. Cleveland, O., 1911. (394 p.)

Previously (1909) published in Denver, Colorado.

Twitchell, R. E. (trans.). The leading facts of New Mexican history. 2 vols. Cleveland, O., 1911-1917.

Translation of documents from the General Land Office in Santa Fé. "Unfortunately," according to J. M. Espinosa, "these translations are full of minor inaccuracies" (*First Expedition of Vargas into New Mexico, 1692*, p. 30, note 18).

Twitchell, R. E. The Spanish archives of New Mexico. 2 vols. Cleveland, O., 1914.

Twitchell, R. E. Spanish colonization in New Mexico in the Oñate and de Vargas periods. Santa Fé: Historical Society of New Mexico, 1919. (39 p.)

Twitchell, R. E. The story of the conquest of Santa Fé, New Mexico, and the building of old Fort Marcy. A.D. 1846. Santa Fé: Historical Society of New Mexico, 1923. (63 p.)

Twitchell, R. E. Colonel Juan Bautista de Anza. Diary of his expedition to the Moquis in 1780, with introduction and notes. Santa Fé: Historical Society of New Mexico, 1918. (44 p.)

Twitchell, R. E. The Palace of the Governors, the city of Santa Fé, its museums and monuments. Santa Fé: Historical Society of New Mexico, 1924. (47 p.)

Twitchell, R. E. "The last campaign of General de Vargas, 1704." OSFé, II (1914), 66-72.

Van Stone, M. R. Spanish folksongs of New Mexico. Chicago, 1928.

Vaughan, J. H. History and government of New Mexico. State College, N. M., 1921. (369 p.)

Venturi, P. T. (ed.). "Nuovo lettere inediti del P. Eusebio Fr. Chino de C. de G." AHSJ, III (1934), 248-264.

Seven letters concerning Kino, 1676-1707.

Vestal, S. The old Santa Fé trail. Boston, 1939. (309 p.)

Vetancurt, A. de. Historia antigua de Mexico. 4 vols. 2nd edition, Mexico, 1870-1871.

The first edition of this work appeared in 1697-98. It contains "Teatro Mexicano" (2 vols.), "Crónica de la Provincia del Santo Evangelio de Mexico" (1 vol.), and "Menologio Franciscano" (1 vol.). The "Cronica" gives information on New Mexico and the "Menologio" biographical sketches of Franciscans who labored in New Mexico as missionaries, in both cases on the basis of documents, many of which have since disappeared.

Vierra, C. New Mexico architecture. AaA, VII (1918).

Villa, E. A. "El protomártir de la Pimería Alta: Francisco Xavier Saeta, fundador de Caborca." DH, II (1940), 111-113.

Villagutierre y Sotomayor, Juan de. Historia de la conquista, perdida y restauración de el reyno y provincias de la Nuevo Mexico en la América Septentrional (c. 1704).

This MS, comprising 890 folios, was never published. According to J. M. Espinosa, Villagutierre drew "two-thirds of his material . . . from the Vargas papers" (*First Expedition of Vargas into New Mexico, 1692*, p. 31). A copy of this MS is also in the Biblioteca Nacional de Madrid, according to Otto Maas who published a study of it and an index of its contents in *Misiones de Nuevo Mexico*, Madrid, 1929, pp. vi-lvi.

Villiers du Terrage, M. de. "La massacre de l'expedition aspagnole du Missouri (II août 1720)." Paris: Journal, Societé des Americanistes, XIII (1921), 239-255.

Vogt, E. Z. "El Moro National monument." Pa, XII (1922), 161-168.

An authentic description of Inscription Rock, discussing the historical data inscribed on it.

Von Wuthenau, A. "The Spanish military chapels in Santa Fé and the reredos of Our Lady of Light." NMHR, X (1935), 175-194.

Wagner, H. R. "New Mexico Spanish press." NMHR, XII (1937), 1-40; also reprint, Historical Society of New Mexico, Santa Fé, 1937. (40 p.)

Wallace, S. E. Land of the Pueblos. New York, 1888. (285 p.)

Walter, P. A. F. The Cities that died of fear. Santa Fé, N. M.

Walter, P. A. F. A New Mexico Lourdes. Pa, 'III (1916), 3-27.

Warner, L. H. "Conveyance of property, the Spanish and Mexican way." NMHR, VI (1931), 334-359.

Watson, E. L. "The cult of the Mountain Lion." Pa, XXXIV (1933), 95-109.

West, E. H. "The right of asylum in New Mexico in the seventeenth and eighteenth centuries." HAHR, VIII (1928), 357-391.

White, L. A. (ed.). Folk dances of the Spanish colonials of New Mexico. 2nd edition, Santa Fé, 1940. (46 p.)

White, L. A. (ed.). Pioneers of American anthropology. The Bandelier-Morgan letters, 1873-1883. 2 vols. Albuquerque, N. M., 1942.

White, L. A. The pueblo of San Felipe. Menasha, Wis.: American Anthropological Association, Memoirs, No. 38. 1932. (69 p.)

White, L. A. The pueblo of Santo Domingo, New Mexico. Menasha, Wis.: American Anthropological Association, Memoirs, No. 43. 1935. (210 p.)

Williston, S. W. and H. T. Martin. "Some pueblo ruins in Scott County, Kansas" Topeka: Kansas Historical Society, Collections, No. VI. 1897-1900. 124-130.

Worcester, D. E. "The beginnings of the Apache menace in the Southwest." NMHR, XVI (1941), 1-14.
Shows that the Apache menace began before the end of the seventeenth century.

Wyllys, R. K. "Padre Luis Velarde's Relación of Pimería Alta, 1716." NMHR, VI (1931), 111-157.

Wyllys, R. K. "A short bibliography of works in English, on the Spanish missions of the Southwest." ArizHR, IV (1932), 58-61.

Wyllys. R. K. "Kino of Pimería Alta, apostle of the Southwest." ArizHR, V (1932), 5-32, 95-134, 205-225, 308-326.

Wyllys, R. K. Pioneer padre: the life and times of Eusebio Francisco Kino. Dallas, Tex., 1935. (230 p.)

VII. CALIFORNIA, 1769-1846

Altamira y Crevea, R. "The share of Spain in the history of the Pacific Ocean." The Pacific Ocean in history (New York, 1917).

Atherton, G. California, an intimate history. New York and London, 1914. (329 p.); New York, 1927. (356 p.)

Atherton, G. The Californians. 2nd edition, London and New York, 1898, 351 p.; 3rd edition, New York, 1908. (351 p.)

Atherton, G. The Dooms woman. New York, 1901. (263 p.)
Historical romance of California.

Atherton, G. Rezanov. New York and London, 1906. (320 p.)

Atherton, G. Rezanov, Nikolai Petrovich, 1764 - 1807. New York, 1919 (255 p.); 2nd edition, New York, 1934 (196 p.)

Atherton, G. Rezanov and Doña Concha. New York, 1937. (218 p.)

Atkinson, F. W. The Argonauts of 1769, a narrative of the occupation of San Diego and Monterey by Don Gaspár de Portolá. Watsonville, Calif., 1936. (166 p.)
Story of the land and sea expeditions that resulted in the occupation of California by Spain.

Baker, A. J. (trans.). "Fray Benito de la Sierra's account of the Hezeta expedition to the northwest coast in 1775." CHSQ, IX (1930), 201-242.

Ballard, H. M. "San Luis Obispo County in Spanish and Mexican times." CHSQ, I (1922), 152-172.

Bancroft, H. H. History of California. 7 vols. San Francisco, 1886-1890.
Valuable for wealth of references to source materials.

Barry, J. N. "Spaniards in early Oregon." WHQ, XXIII (1932), 25-34.
The account begins with the year 1725.

Bartlett, J. R. Personal narrative of explorations and incidents. 2 vols. New York, 1854.
Bartlett visited California in 1852

Beechey, F. W. Narrative of a voyage to the Pacific and Beering's strait . . . in the years 1825-26-27-28. 2 vols. London, 1831.
Beechey visited California in 1826.

Cheney, K. B. (comp.). Swinging the censer. Santa Barbara, Calif., 1931. (287 p.)
"Reminiscences of old Santa Barbara, by Katherine M. Bell" (subtitle).

Berger, J. A. The Franciscan missions of California. New York, 1941. (392 p.)

Bolton, H. E. "The early explorations of Father Garcés on the Pacific slope." The Pacific Ocean in history (New York, 1917).

Bolton, H. E. (ed.). Historical memoirs of New California, by Fray Francisco Palóu, O.F.M. 4 vols. Berkeley: University of California press, 1926. (331, 390, 398, 446 pp.)
An excellent translation of Palóu's *Noticias de Nueva California* with a scholarly study of "Palóu and his Writings" (pp. xxi-xc).

Bolton, H. E. (ed.). Fray Juan Crespi, missionary explorer on the Pacific coast, 1769-1774. Berkeley: University of California press, 1927. (402 p.)
Translation of four Crespi documents (letters and diaries) concerning the Portolá, the Fages, and the Pérez expeditions, with a valuable study of "Fray Juan Crespi, Missionary Explorer" (xi-lxi) and "The Crespi Manuscripts" (pp. lxii-lxiv).

Bolton, H. E. (ed.). Anza's California expeditions. 5 vols. Berkeley: University of California Press, 1930. (520, 473, 436, 552, 426 pp.)

A work of high scholarship and inestimable value. Vol. I, entitled "Outpost of Empire," is "a vigorous narrative by Professor Bolton of the Anza expeditions to California and the founding of San Francisco. Vol. II, "Opening a Land Route to California," and Vol. III, "The San Francisco Colony," comprise the diaries of Anza, Diaz, and Fathers Garcés, Font, and Eixarch Vol. IV, also entitled "The San Francisco Colony," contains the complete diary of Father Font. Vol. V, entitled "Correspondence," contains the official and personal correspondence of the two Anza expeditions.

Bolton, H. E. (ed.). Font's complete diary. A chronicle of the founding of San Francisco. Berkeley: University of California press, 1933. (552 p.)

Separate issue of Vol. IV of the author's *Anza's California Expeditions*. This day by day record of Font, to quote Bolton, is "a superb diary—one of the best in all Western Hemisphere history, it is safe to say."

Bolton, H. E. A Pacific coast pioneer. Berkeley: University of California press, 1927. (64 p.)

A separate issue of the introduction to the author's *Fray Juan Crespi, Missionary Explorer on the Pacific Coast, 1769-1774*.

Bolton, H. E. Outpost of empire. The story of the founding of San Francisco. New York, 1931. (334 p.)

A separate issue of Vol. I of *Anza's California Expeditions*.

Bolton, H. E. Cross, sword and gold pan. Los Angeles, 1936. (31 p.)

A series of brief historical essays interpreting "a group of notable full-cover paintings depicting outstanding episodes in the exploration and settlement of the West, by Carl Oscar Borg and Millard Sheets" (subtitle).

Bolton, H. E. (ed.). "Expedition to San Francisco Bay in 1770:

Diary of Pedro Fages." San Francisco: Academy of Pacific Coast History, Publications, No. II (1911), 141-159.

Bolton, H. E. "The Iturbide revolution in the Californias." HAHR, II (1919), 188-242.

Bolton, H. E. "In the South San Joaquín ahead of Garcés." CHSQ, X (1931), 211-219.

Bolton, H. E. "Drake's plate of brass." CHSQ, XVI (1941), 1-16.

Bowman, M. M. "The first printer in California." LofS, III (1903), 30-31.

Brebner, J. B. "Why the Spaniards temporarily abandoned Nootka Sound in 1789." CanHR, XVII (1936), 168-178.

Estévan Josef Martínez had occupied Nootka Sound for the Spaniards.

Brown, K. F. The California missions. San Francisco, 1939. (64 p.)

Bynum, L. (trans.). "Governor Don Felipe de Neve: a chronological note of Felipe de Neve and his governorship of the Californias [1775-1783]." Southern California Historical Society Publications, XV (1931), pt. 1, 63-68.

Translation of four reports by Governor Neve.

Calzada, Juan. "Respuesta del R. P. Guardian Fr. Juan Calzada al Excelentísimo señor Virrey, dandole las razones por las que no han sido entregadas a las Jurisdicciones Real Ordinaria y Eclesiástica, las misiones de la Alta California." Las Misiones de la Alta California, Mexico: Colección de Documentos Históricos, 1914, pp. 197-254.

The document refers to the transfer of the California mission by the Franciscans in 1821.

Camp, C. L. (ed.). "The journal of a 'crazy man', travels and scenes in California from the year 1834 to the American conquest, the narrative of Albert Ferdinand Morris." CHSQ, XV (1936), 103-138, 225-241.

Carreño, A. M. (ed.). Noticias de Nutka . . . por D. Joseph Mariano Moziño Suarez de Figueroa. Año de 1793. Mexico, D. F.: Sociedad Mexicana de Geografía y Estadística, 1913. (117 p.)
Moziño accompanied, as botanist, the expedition to Nootka Sound in 1793. This edition of his *Noticias* is preceded by a critical study by the editor.

Carrasco y Guisasola, F. Documentos referentes al reconocimiento desde el Cabo de San Lucas al de Mendocino, recopilados en el Archivo de Indias. Madrid, 1882.
The volume contains documents between the dates 1584 and 1609. Most of them concern the voyage of Vizcaíno, three of which are translated by George Butler Griffin in Historical Society of Southern California Publications, II (1891), 5-73.

Carter, C. F. (trans.). "Duhaut-Cilly's account of California in the years 1827-28." CHSQ, VIII (1929); 130-166, 214-250, 306-356.

Carter, C. F. The missions of Nueva California. San Francisco, 1900. (189 p.)

Caughey, J. W. History of the Pacific coast. Los Angeles, priv. print. 1933. (429 p.)
"This book is the first attempt to relate the history of the entire Pacific coast of North America." (Preface.)

Caughey, J. W. California. New York, 1940. (680 p.)
A masterly, thorough, and charming book—to date the best comprehensive history of California.

Chapman, C. E. "The founding of San Francisco." The Pacific Ocean in history (New York, 1917).

Chapman, C. E. The founding of Spanish California: the northwestward expansion of New Spain, 1687-1783. New York, 1916. (485 p.)

Chapman, C. E. "Sebastián Vizcaíno: exploration of California." SHQ, XXIII (1919), 285-301.

Chapman, C. E. "The Alta California supply ships, 1773-1776." SHQ, XIX (1916), 184-194.

Chapman, C. E. A history of California: the Spanish period. New York, 1921. (527 p.)
Contains (pp. 487-509) a valuable bibliography of California history.

Chapman, C. E. "Difficulties in maintaining the department of San Blas, 1775-1777." SHQ, XIX (1916), 261-270.

Chapman, C. E. Diario of Fray Narciso Durán to the Sacramento River in 1817. Berkeley: University of California Press, 1911. (21 p.)

Chapman, C. E. "The literature of California history." SHQ, XXII (1919), 318-352.
For "a correction" see SHQ, XXIII (1920), 78.

Chapman, C. E. "A great Franciscan in California: Fermín Francisco de Lasuén." CHR, V (1919), 131-155.

Chapman, C. E. "Gali and Rodríquez Cermenho: exploration of California." SHQ, XXIII (1920), 204-213.

Chase, J. S. and C. F. Saunders. The California padres and their missions. Boston, 1915. (417 p.)

Chinard, G. Le voyage de Laperouse sur les côtes de l'Alaska et de la Californie: 1786. Baltimore: Johns Hopkins University press, 1937. (144 p.)

Clarke, A. B. Travels in Mexico and California. Boston, 1852. (138 p.)

Cleland, R. C. Pathfinders. Los Angeles, 1929. (452 p.)
Deals with the early explorations in California in the light of the original narratives.

Clinch, B. J. California and its missions: their history to the treaty of Guadalupe Hidalgo. 2 vols. San Francisco, 1904.

Colton, W. Three years in California. New York, 1850. (456 p.)
Covers the years 1846-1849.

Corcoran, M. S. "Mission San Juan Bautista." M-A, XII (1930), 246-259.

Cowan, R. E. A bibliography of the history of California and the Pacific Midwest (1510-1906). San Francisco, 1914 (318 p.); 2nd edition, (1510-1930), 3 vols. 1933.

Coy, O. C. "Josiah Gregg in California." New Spain and the Anglo-American West. Los Angeles, Calif., 1932. II, 185-214.

Cutts, J. M. The conquest of New Mexico and California by the forces of the United States in the years 1846 and 1847. Philadelphia, 1847. (264 p.)

Dakin, S. B. (ed.). A Scotch paisano, Hugo Reid's life in California, 1832-1852. Berkeley. University of California press, 1939. (312 p.)

Dale, H. C. (ed.). The Ashley-Smith explorations and discovery of a central route to the Pacific, 1822-1829, Cleveland, 1918; 352 p.; 2nd edition, Glendale, Calif., 1941. (360 p.)
Contains the original journals of the expeditions which reached California and visited some of the southern missions, where they were well received by the Franciscan missionaries.

Dana, R. H. Two years before the mast. New York, 1840. (432 p.) Later editions: New York, 1899; Boston and New York, 1911.
Dana visited California in 1835 as a boy on the *Pilgrim*.

Dane, G. E. (trans.). "The founding of the presidio and mission of our Holy Father St. Francis, etc." CHSQ, XIV (1935), 102-110.
This is a translation of chapter 45 of Palóu's biography of Fray Junípero Serra.

D'Auteroche, C. Voyage to California to observe the transit of Venus. London, 1778. (215 p.)
The scientific expedition visited northern Mexico, sections of the Southwest, and California.

Davidson, G. The discovery of San Francisco Bay; also Francis Drake on the Northwest coast of America. San Francisco, 1907. (153 p.)

Davis, C. C. "Ramona, the ideal and the real." OW, XIX (1905), 575-596.

Davis, J. F. "The history of California." The Pacific Ocean in history (New York, 1917).

Davis, N. The old missions of California: the history of the peaceful conquest of the state. Oakland, 1926. (118 p.)

Dawson, G. S. California: story of our Southwest corner. New York, 1939. (212 p.)

Dellenbaugh, F. S. The romance of the Colorado River. New York, 3rd edition, 1909. (401 p.)

Dellenbaugh, F. S. Fremont and '49: story of a remarkable career. New York, 1914. (547 p.)

Denis, A. J. Spanish Alta California. New York, 1927. (437 p.)
The story of the Spaniards on the Pacific coast.

Document. "The Fremont episode." CHSQ, IV (1925), 81-87, 374-381.
A series of letters and documents of the year 1846 regarding Fremont's campaign in California.

Document. "Spanish missions in California, 1769-1834." JAH, XVII (1923), 131-141.

Document. "The Bear Flag movement." CHSQ, I (1922), 72-95, 178-191.

Documents bearing on the movement.

Document. Las misiones de la Alta California. Mexico: Archivo y Biblioteca de la Secretaria de Hacienda. Colección de Documentos Históricos. II. 1914. (269 p.)

Contains six important documents bearing on California and its missions.

Document. "Informe que dió el Exmo. señor Marqués de Sonora cuando estuvo en Californias al Exmo. señor virrey de Mexico Marqués de Croix, manifestando le que son dichas Californias [1772]. Mexico, D. F.: Boletín del Archivo General de la Nación, IV (1933), 806-832.

Official report of José de Gálvez to the viceroy on his inspection tour in Lower California.

Document. "Exploration and plans for the settlement of California." Bolton, H. E.: Spanish Exploration in the Southwest, 1542-1706, 1-134.

Contains the "Relation of the Voyage of Juan Rodríguez Cabrillo," the "Diary of Sebastián Vizcaíno," and the "Report of Father Ascensión."

Document. ["The founding of Los Angeles"], Los Angeles: Southern California Historical Society, Publications, XV (1931), pt. 1, 117-263.

Document. "Año de 1602—El cura Vicario de Acapulco, con la parte del Convento de Carmelitas Descalzos, sobre la pertenencia de derechos del funeral hecho por los que murieron en el descubrimiento de las Californias, que el General Vizcayno hizo hasta el Cabo Mendicino." Mexico, D. F.: Las Misiones de la Alta California, pp. 7-26.

Document. ["The Fremont episode in California"], CHSQ, I-VIII (1922-1929).

The documents appeared serially without interruption through the first eight volumes of the *California Historical Society Quarterly.*

Document. "Reglamento para el gobierno de la Provincia de California (October 24, 1781)." LofS, VI (1897), 77-82.

English translation of the important document. It was printed in Mexico in 1784 by Felipe de Zúñiga y Ontiveros.

Document. [Report of Viceroy Revilla Gigedo.] LofS, XI (1902), 32-41, 105-112, 168-173, 225-233, 283-289.

Document. "Diary of Miguel Costansó." LofS, XIV (1905), XV (1906), 38-49.

Document. "Diary of Fray Junípero Serra." OW, XVI (1902), 293-296, 399-406, 513-518, 635-642; XVII (1903), 69-76.

Describes the expedition of Portolá from Loreto in Lower California to San Diego, Upper California, March 28-June 30, 1769. Here translated for the first time from the photograph copy (35 pp.) in the E. Ayer Collection, Newberry Library, Chicago, Ill. The Franciscan Missionaries of Mary, North Providence, R. I., published a translation of the diary (64 p.) in 1936.

Document. "Manifiesto que el Discretorio del Apostólico Colegio de San Fernando hizo al Rey, en 26 de febrero de 1776, sobre los nuevos descubrimientos de la Alta California." Las Misiones de la Alta California, pp. 29-85.

Document. "Informe del Administrador del Fondo Piadoso de Californias al Presidente de la Federación. [Mexico, March 6, 1825.]" Las Misiones de la Alta California, pp. 257-267.

Document. "Parecer formado por el padre Domingo Rivas, a petición de D. Joaquín Cortina, en repulsa del informe dado a S.M. sobre mejoras de la Nueva California." Las Misiones de la Alta California, pp. 119-194.

Duflot de Mofras, M. Exploration du territoire de L'Oregon, des Californies, et de la Mar Vermeille . . . 2 vols. Paris, 1844. (See below under M. E. Wilbur.)
Duflot de Mofras visited California in 1841.

Duhaut-Cilly, A. Voyage autour du monde, principalment a la Californie et aux Iles Sandwich, pendant les années 1826, 1827, 1828, et 1829. 2 vols. Paris. 1834-1835.
For the English translation see above under C. F. Carter.

Dunne, P. M. Pioneer Black Robes on the west coast. Berkeley: University of California press, 1940. (286 p.)
The story of Jesuit missionary labors in western Sonora and Lower California.

Dwinelle, J. M. Colonial history of the city of San Francisco. San Francisco, 1866. (391 p.)

Elder, P. The old Spanish missions of California. San Francisco, 1914. (89 p.)

Eldredge, J. S. The beginnings of San Francisco, from the expedition of Anza, 1774, to the city charter of April 15, 1850. 2 vols. San Francisco, 1912.

Eldredge, Z. S. (ed.). History of California. 5 vols. New York, 1915.

Eldredge, Z. S. "Studies of the Anza route." JAH, II (1908), 38-42, 255-261, 521-526, 696-701; III (1909), 103-112, 171-179, 395-402.

Ellison, W. H. "The federal Indian policy in California, 1846-1860." MVHR, IX (1922), 36-67.

Ellison, W. H. "History of Vera Cruz Island grant." PHR, VI (1937), 270-283.

Ellison, J. "California and the nation, 1846-1869: a study of the federal relations of a frontier community." SHQ, XXX (1926), 83-113.

Ellison, J. "The mineral land question in California, 1848-1866." SHQ, XXX (1926), 34-55.

Elwood, L. B. Queen Calafia's land. New York, 1940. (108 p.)
A popular account of California's history.

Emory, W. H. Notes of a military reconnaisance of New Mexico and California. Washington, 1848. (614 p.)
Account of expedition from Leavenworth to San Diego.

Engelhardt, Z. "Interrogatorio y respuesta of Fr. José Señan." CHR, V (1919), 55-66.

Engelhardt, Z. The Franciscans in California. Harbor Springs, Mich., 1897. (516 p.)
Now superseded by the author's larger 4-volume work on the California missions.

Engelhardt, Z. Missions and Missionaries of California. 5 vols. (5th vol., Index), San Francisco, I (1908; 2nd ed., 1929), II (1912; 2nd ed., 1930); III (1913); IV (1915); V (1916). (654 [784], 682 [706], 663, 817, 160 pp.)
The standard work on the history of the California missions during the Spanish and Mexican régimes; based on primary sources, manuscript and printed; intended as a reference work rather than for the general reader.

Engelhardt, Z. The holy man of Santa· Clara, or life, virtues, and miracles of Fr. Magín Catalá, O.F.M. San Francisco, 1909. (203 p.)

Engelhardt, Z. San Diego Mission. San Francisco, 1920. (358 p.)

Engelhardt, Z. San Luis Rey Mission. San Francisco, 1921. (265 p.)

Engelhardt, Z. San Juan Capistrano Mission, Los Angeles, 1922. (259 p.)

96

Engelhardt, Z. Santa Barbara Mission. San Francisco, 1923. (470 p.)

Engelhardt, Z. San Francisco, or Mission Dolores. Chicago: Franciscan Herald press, 1924. (432 p.)

Engelhardt, Z. San Gabriel Mission and the beginnings of Los Angeles. San Gabriel, Calif., 1927. (369 p.)

Engelhardt, Z. San Fernando Rey, the Mission of the Valley. Chicago: Franciscan Herald press, 1927. (160 p.)

Engelhardt, Z. San Antonio de Padua, the Mission of the Sierras. Santa Barbara, Calif., 1929. (140 p.)

Engelhardt, Z. Mission Nuestra Señora de la Soledad. Santa Barbara, Calif., 1929. (88 p.)

Engelhardt, Z. San Buenaventura, the Mission by the Sea. Santa Barbara, Calif., 1930. (170 p.)

Engelhardt, Z. Mission San Juan Bautista. Santa Barbara, Calif., 1931. (153 p.)

Engelhardt, Z. San Miguel, Arcangel, the Mission on the Highway. Santa Barbara, Calif., 1931. (92 p.)

Engelhardt, Z. Mission Santa Inés, Virgin and Martyr, and its ecclesiastical seminary. Santa Barbara, Calif. 1932. (200 p.)

Engelhardt, Z. Mission La Concepción Purísima de Maria Santísima. Santa Barbara, Calif., 1932. (131 p.)

Engelhardt, Z. Mission San Luís Obispo in the Valley of the Bears. Santa Barbara, Calif., 1933. (218 p.)

Engelhardt, Z. Mission San Carlos Borromeo. Santa Barbara, Calif., 1934. (264 p.)

Espinosa, A. M. "Spanish folktales from California." Hpa, XXIII (1940), 121-144.

Farnham, E. W. California indoors and out. New York, 1856. (508 p.)

Farnham, J. T. The early days in California. Philadelphia, 1859. (314 p.)

Farquhar, F. P. "Spanish discovery of the Sierra Nevada." San Francisco, Calif.: Sierra Club, Bulletin, XIII (1928), No. 1, 54-61.
Discusses three Spanish expeditions: Anza (1775-1776) Moraga (1806), and Arguello (1817).

Fernández, Justino (ed.). Tomás de Suría y su viaje con Malaspina, 1791. Mexico, 1939. (134 p.)
The diary of the official artist accompanying the Malapina expedition in search of a strait from Acapulco, in Mexico, to Alaska. H. R. Wagner published an English translation.

Field, M. A. Chimes of mission bells. San Francisco, 1914. (79 p.)
A brief, popular sketch of California and its missions.

Fita y Colomé, F. (ed.). Historia de la California, obra anónima del P. Andrés Marcos Burriel . . . datos inéditos e ilustrativos de su composición, aprobación y edición. Madrid: Real Academia de la Historia, Boletín, LII (1908), 396-438.
Andrés Burriel, S. J., published his Noticia anonymously in 1757.

Fitch, A. H. Junípero Serra, the man and his work. Chicago, 1914. (364 p.)

Flint, T. (ed.). The personal narrative, by J. O. Pattie. Chicago, 1930. (428 p.)

Ford, T. L. Dawn and the dons: the romance of Monterey. San Francisco, 1926. (236 p.)

Forbes, A. S. C. California missions and landmarks. 8th edition. Los Angeles, 1925.
The first edition appeared in 1903.

Forbes, A. S. C. Mission tales in the days of the dons. Chicago, 1909.

Forbes, A. California: A history of upper and lower California. San Francisco, 1937. (229 p.)
This is a reprint, with an introduction by H. I. Priestley, of the London, 1839, edition.

Fremont, J. C. Report of the exploring expedition to the Rocky Mountains in the year 1842, and to Oregon and North California in the years 1843-1844. Washington, 1845. (583 p.)

Fremont, J. C. Exploring expedition to the Rocky Mountains. Buffalo, N. Y., 1849. (278 p.)

Frost, J. History of the State of California. Pasadena, 1859. (508 p.)

Galbraith, E. C. "Malapina's voyage around the world." CHSQ, III (1924), 238-244.
Deals mainly with exploration along the California coast.

Geary, G. J. The secularization of the California missions, 1810-1846. Washington, D. C.: Catholic University of America press, 1934. (204 p.)

Gleesen, W. History of the Catholic Church in California. 2 vols. San Francisco, 1871.

Golder, F. A. Russian expansion on the Pacific, 1641-1850. Cleveland, 1914. (368 p.)

Goodwin, C. John Charles Fremont, an explanation of his career. Stanford, Calif.: Stanford University press, 1930. (285 p.)

Goodwin, C. (ed.). Thomas Oliver Larkin: description of California. Los Angeles: New Spain and the Anglo-American West, Los Angeles, 1932, II, 103-119.
Larkin's description of California is dated June 15, 1846.

Gray, A. A. History of California from 1542. New York, 1934. (655 p.)
Thirteen chapters deal with the period before the American conquest.

Greenhow, R. The history of Oregon and California, and the other territories of the northwest coast of North America. 4th edition. Boston, 1847. (492 p.)

Griffin, G. B. (trans. and ed.). Documents from the Sutro Collection. Historical Society of Southern California, Publications, 1891. (213 p.)
Contains thirteen documents, concerning California, from 1584 to 1774.

Hague, E. Early Spanish-California folksongs. New York, 1922. (115 p.)

Hall, T. California trails: intimate guide to the Old Missions. New York, 1920. (243 p.)

Hanna, P. T. California through four centuries. New York, 1935. (212 p.)
A handy "Who's Who" in California history, with data arranged chronologically.

Hanna, P. T. Chinigchinich, by Fray Gerónimo Boscana. Santa Ana, Calif., 1933. (247 p.)
"A revised and annotated version of Alfred Robinson's translation of Father Geronimo Boscana's historical account of the belief, usages, customs and extravagancies of the Indians of this mission of San Juan Capistrano, called the Acagchemem tribe" (subtitle). Boscana's account was published originally by Alfred Robinson in his *Life in California* (New York, 1846).

Harrington, J. P. (trans. and ed.). A new original version of Boscana's historical account of the San Juan Capistrano Indians of Southern California. Washington, D. C.: Smithsonian Institution, 1934. (62 p.)
Translation with introduction of Father Boscana's *Chinigchinich.* The translation is from "the recently discovered manuscript consisting of an 1822 variant of Boscana's historical account as published in English in Alfred Robinson's *Life in California* (New York, 1846)" (Griffin: *Writings,* 1934, p. 34.)

Heizer, R. F. and W. W. Elmen-dorf. "Francis Drake's California anchorage in the light of the Indian language spoken there." PHR, XI (1942), 213-217.

Hemert-Engert, A. van and F. J. Teggart (eds.). "The narrative of the Portolá expedition of 1769-1770 . . . " Berkeley, Calif.: Academy of Pacific Coast History, Publications, I (1910), 91-159.

Hendry, G. W. "Francisco Palóu's boundary marker: a record of the discovery of the first boundary between Upper and Lower California." CHSQ, V (1926), 321-327.
Discusses the line established in 1773 marking the boundary between the Lower California Dominican and the Upper California Franciscan missions.

Hill, J. J. History of Warner's Ranch and its environs. Los Angeles, 1927. (221 p.)

Hittell, T. H. History of California. 4 vols. San Francisco, 1885-1897.

Holway, M. G. The art of the old world in New Spain and the mission days of Alta California. San Francisco, 1922. (172 p.)

Hunt, R. D. California the golden. New York, 1911. (362 p.)

Hunt, R. D. (ed.). California and Californians. 5 vols. Los Angeles, 1926.
Volume I, written by Nellie Van de Grift Sánchez, deals with the Spanish period.

Jackson, H. H. A century of dishonor. New York, 1881. (457 p.); 2nd ed., Boston, 1888. (514 p.)
"A sketch of the United States Government's dealings with some of the Indian tribes" (subtitle).

Jackson, H. H. Ramona, a story. Boston, 1901. (490 p.)
A well-wrought and fascinating historical novel on conditions in colonial California.

Jackson. H. H. Glimpses of California and the missions. Boston, 1902. (292 p.)
A well-written and remarkably correct picture of Spanish mission days in California. First edition appeared in 1883 and was reprinted in 1886.

Jackson, H. H. Father Junípero and the mission Indians of California. Boston, 1902. (159 p.)
A re-issue of chapters I and II of the author's *Glimpses of California and the missions.*

James, G. W. In and out of the old missions of California. Boston, 1905; 2nd ed., 1914. (392 p.)
A new and revised edition (392 p.) was published in Boston in 1927.

James, G. W. Through Ramona's country. Boston, 1908. (406 p.)

James, G. W. The old Franciscan missions of California. Boston, 1913. (287 p.); 2nd edition, 1925. (260 p.)

James, G. W. and C. S. Williams (ed. and trans.). Francisco Palóu's Life and Apostolic Labors of the Venerable Father Junípero Serra, Founder of the Franciscan Missions of California. Pasadena, Calif., 1913, publ. priv., (338 p.)
From the Spanish edition published in Mexico in 1787. When using this translation, it should be checked with the original Spanish text.

James, G. W. California romantic and beautiful. Boston, 1914. (433 p.)

James, G. W. Fremont in California. Los Angeles, 1903. (32 p.)

James, G. W. Heroes of California. Boston, 1910. (515 p.)

James, G. W. Old missions and mission Indians of California. Los Angeles, Calif., 1895. (124 p.)

James, G. W. Picturesque Pala. Pasadena, Calif., 1916. (82 p.)

James, G. W. The lake of the sky. Pasadena, Calif., 1915. (395 p.); 2nd edition, 1921 (395 p.); 3rd edition, 1928 (351 p.)

A history of Lake Tahoe in Sierra of California and Nevada.

Jane, C. (trans.). A Spanish voyage to Vancouver and the northwest coast of America. London, 1930. (142 p.)

Translation from the Spanish with introduction of "the narrative of the voyage made in the year 1792 by the schooners Sutil and Mexicana to explore the strait of Fuca" (subtitle). The Spanish edition was published in Madrid, in 1802.

Kirchhoff, P. and P. R. Heinrichs (ed. and trans.). Noticias de la península Americana de California. Mexico, 1942.

First translation into Spanish from the original German (Mannheim, 1772) of treatise by the Jesuit missionary, Juan Jacobo Baegert on the anthropology, ethnology, and other affairs in Lower California.

Kotzebue, O. von. A voyage of discovery into the South Sea and Bering's Straits. 3 vols. London, 1821.

The author visited San Francisco in 1816. What he reports regarding the California missions is based on hearsay from Mexican officials, having himself seen little of the missions.

Kroeber, A. L. Handbook of the Indians of California. Washington, D. C.: Government Printing Office, 1925. (995 p.)

The standard work on the subject.

Kuykendall, R. S. "An American shipbuilder for Spanish California." HAHR, V (1922), 90-92.

Lake, S. E. and A. A. Gray (trans. and eds.). The history of California, by Francisco Javier Clavijero. Stanford, Calif.: Stanford University press, 1938. (413 p.)

From the original Italian, dealing with Lower California.

Langsdorff, G. H. Voyages and travels. 4 vols. London, 1813.

Description of travels made during the years 1803-1807, during which Langsdorff visited the missions in the San Francisco Bay region.

La Perouse, J. F. G. de. Voyage around the world, 1785-1788. London, 1798 (3 vols.); Edinburgh, 1798, an abridged edition. (336 p.); London, 1801, an abridged edition. (333 p.)

Lummis, C. F. "Old art in California." OW, XXI (1907), 212-230.

A study of backgrounds with illustrations.

Lummis, C. F. (trans.). "The Informe of Count de Revilla Gigedo." LofS, XI (1899), 32-41; 105-112, 168-174, 225-234, 283-290.

The report is dated April 12, 1793, dealing with California and expeditions to the northwest coast, to the year 1793.

Lummis, C. F. Spanish songs of old California. New York, 1929.

Lummis, C. F. The Spanish pioneers and the California missions. Chicago, 1929. (343 p.)

A revised and enlarged edition of the author's earlier work, *The Spanish pioneers.*

Marshall, T. M. "Stockton's proclamation to the San Diego insurgents." SHQ, XX (1916), 151-153.

McCoy, W. J. Folksongs of Spanish California. San Francisco, 1926.

McDonald, W. E. "The Pious Fund of the Californias." CHR, XIX (1934), 427-436.

McGroarty, J. S. California, its history and romance. Los Angeles, 1911. (393 p.)

A literary classic, dealing with the Spanish and the Mexican period. A seventh edition appeared in 1920.

McGroarty, J. S. (ed.). History of Los Angeles County. 3 vols. Chicago, 1923.

Maloney, A. B. "Hudson's Bay Company in California." OHQ, XXXVII (1936), 9-23.

Commercial and political activities between the years 1825 and 1845.

Manning, W. R. "The Nootka Sound controversy." Washington, D. C.: American Historical Association, Annual Report, 1905, 279-478.

Miller, M. Harbor of the sun. New York, 1940. (329 p.)
Deals with San Diego, California, colonial and modern period; popular in approach and treatment.

Morrison, G. Bells: their history and romance. Santa Barbara, Calif., 1932. (347 p.)

Mosk, S. A. "Price-fixing in Spanish California." CHSQ, XVII (1938), 118-122.
Covers the years 1781-1803, on the basis of new original materials.

Muller, S. "The apostle of California." Th, IX (1934), 458-476.

Murphy, T. D. On sunset highways. Boston, 1921, revised edition. (376 p.)

Nasatir, A. P. (ed.). "The French consulate in California." CHSQ, XI-XIII (1932-1934).

Newcomb, R. The old mission churches and historic homes of California: their history, architecture, art, and lore. Philadelphia, 1925. (379 p.)

North, A. W. The mother of California. New York, 1908. (169 p.)
Deals with Lower California.

Norton, H. K. Story of California. Chicago, 1913. (390 p.)

Ogden, A. "Hides and Tallow: McCulloch, Hartwell and Company, 1822-1828." CHSQ, VI (1927), 254-264.
Activities of an English business firm in Monterey, 1822-1828.

Ogden, A. "The Californias in Spain's Pacific otter trade, 1775-1795." PHR, I (1931), 444-469.

Ogden, A. The California sea otter trade, 1784-1848. Berkeley: University of California press, 1941.

O'Hagan, T. "The poetry and romance of the Spanish Missions." ACQR, XLVI (1921), 156-165.

Older, C. M. B. California missions and their romances. New York, 1938. (314 p.)

Older, C. M. B. Love stories of old California. New York, 1940. (306 p.)

Ortega, José de. Apostólicos afanes de la Compañia de Jesús. Barcelona, 1754. (452 p.)

Packman, A. Bégué de. Early California hospitality. Glendale, Calif., 1938. (182 p.)
Deals with cookery customs in Spanish California, with recipes and menus of the period. The author traces her ancestry down to the days of Junípero Serra.

Palóu, F. Relación histórica de la vida y apostólicas tareas del Venerable Padre Fray Junípero Serra . . . Mexico, 1787. (See No. 1371.)
Father Palóu was active in California from 1773 to 1786. The value of his biography of Father Serra lies in the fact that he was on intimate terms with his former teacher before and after their arrival and missionary labors in Mexico and both Californias.

Pattie, J. O. Personal narrative. Cleveland, 1905. (380 p.)
This is the R. G. Thwaites edition included in the *Early Western Travels* series. The first edition, prepared by T. Flint, appeared in 1833.

Peatfield, J. J. "Mission music and musicians." LofS, VIII (1895).

Peixotto, E. Romantic California. New York, 1927. New and enlarged edition. (272 p.)

Porter, V. M. General Stephen W. Kearny. Los Angeles, 1911. (35 p.)

Powers, L. B. Old Monterey: California's adobe capital. San Francisco, 1934. (299 p.)

Priestley, H. I. "The Pedro Fages MS. on California." CHR, IV (1919), 486-509; V (1920), 71-90.

Priestley, H. I. A historical, political, and natural description of California by Pedro Fages, soldier of Spain. Berkeley: University of California press, 1937. (83 p.)
Appeared earlier in the *Catholic Historical Review*.

Priestley, H. I. (ed.). "The Colorado River campaign, 1781-1782; diary of Pedro Fages." Berkeley: Academy of Pacific Coast History, Publications, No. 3 (1913), 132-233.

Priestley, H. I. "The reforms of Joseph Galvez in New Spain." The Pacific Ocean in history (New York, 1917).

Priestley, H. I. "Franciscan exploration of California." CHR, VI (1920), 139-155.

Remandino, P. C. The Mediterranean shores of America, Southern California. Philadelphia, 1892:

Repplier, A. Junípero Serra, pioneer colonist of California. New York, 1933. (312 p.)

Richman, I. B. California under Spain and Mexico. New York, 1911. (541 p.)

Roberson, M. Y. (trans.). "Guzmán's 'Breve Noticia'." CHSQ, V (1926), 209-215.
The description, 1828, is important, being an official report on the missions in California at the time of their secularization.

Robinson, A. Life in California, New York. 1846.
Contains Father Boscana's *Chinigchinich*.

Rodríguez de San Miguel, J. Documentos relativos al Piodoso Fondo de Misiones. Mexico, 1845.

Rose, R. S. Diario of the San Carlos by Captain Vicente Vila. Berkeley: University of California press, 1911. (119 p.)
The *diario* relates the incidents from day to day on the voyage from La Paz, Lower California, to San Diego in 1768-1769.

Ross, Mary. "Writings and cartography of Herbert Eugene Bolton." New Spain and the Anglo-American West. Los Angeles, Calif., 1932, II, 245-252.

Rowland, D. "Spanish occupation of the island of Old Providence or Santa Catalina, 1641-1670." HAHR, XV (1935), 298-312.

Royce, J. California. Boston, 1886; 2nd edition, 1914. (513 p.)

Russel, T. C. (ed.). The Rezanov voyage to Nueva California in 1806. San Francisco, 1926. (104 p.)
A revised English translation with corrections and notes by the editor. Count Nikolai Petrovich Rezanov was Russian ambassador and plenipotentiary.

Russel, T. C. (ed.). Life in California, by Alfred Robinson. San Francisco, 1925. (316 p.)
Reprint of Robinson's work first published in New York in 1846, containing also Boscana's *Chinigchinich* from a manuscript which Robinson received as a gift from Father Boscana while visiting at Mission San Juan Capistrano.

Russel, T. C. (trans.). Langsdorff's Narrative of the Rezanov voyage to Nueva California in 1806. San Francisco, 1927. (158 p.)
". . . being that division of Doctor George H. von Langsdorf's Bemerkungen auf einer Reise um die Welt, when as personal physician, he accompanied Rezanov to Nueva California from Sitka, Alaska, and back" (subtitle).

Ryan, J. J. "The Franciscan missions of California." M-A, IX (1926), 134-150.

Sánchez, N. van de Grift. Spanish Arcadia. Los Angeles, 1929. (413 p.)
In the series *California*, edited by J. R. McCarthy (San Francisco, 1929).

Saunders, C. F. and St. John O'Sullivan. Capistrano nights. New York, 1930. (202 p.)

Saunders, C. F. Little book of California missions. New York, (1939). (64 p.)

Saunders, C. F. Southern sierras of California. London, 1923. (367 p.)

Schurz, W. L. "The Manila galleon and California." SHQ, XXI (1917), 107-126.

Silva, O. da. Mission music of California. Los Angeles, 1941. (136 p.)

Simpson, L. B. (trans.). California in 1792: the expedition of José Longinos Martínez. San Marino, Calif.: Huntington Library, Publication, 1938. (111 p.)

Simpson, L. B. "The story of José Longinos Martínez, California's first naturalist." HAHR, XX (1940), 642-649.

Smith, D. E. and F. J. Teggard (eds.). The diary of Gaspár de Portolá. Berkeley: Academy of Pacific Coast History, Publications, I (1909), 31-89.

Smith, F. R. "The burial place of Father Junípero Serra." Hpa, VII (1924), 285-298.

Smith, F. R. "The Spanish missions, of California." Hpa, VII (1924), 243-258.

Smith, F. R. The mission of San Antonio de Padua. Stanford, Calif.: Stanford University press, 1932. (108 p.)

Smythe, W. E. History of San Diego, 1543-1907. San Diego, Calif., 1907. (736 p.); 2nd edition, 2 vols., 1908.

Steck, F. B. "Junípero Serra, pioneer and missionary." FR, XXXVIII (1931), 97-99.

Steck, F. B. "Junípero Serra and the military heads of California." FR, XXVIII (1921). 451-453; XXIX (1922), 8-9, 29-32, 49-51, 70-72, 87-91.

Steele, J. Old California days. Chicago, 1889.

Stephens, H. M. "The conflict of European nations in the Pacific." The Pacific Ocean in history (New York, 1917).

Sugranes, E. The Old Mission San Gabriel. Los Angeles, 1921. (104 p.)

Tamariz, F. de P. "Memoria que presenta al Rey N.S. el teniente de navío D. Francisco de Paula Tamariz, sobre mejorar el sistema de gobierno de la Alta California. Real orden de 5 de julio de 1814. Carta del Virrey Calleja a los Gobernadores de las Californias. Aviso de recibo de la real orden citada." Mexico, D. F.: Las Misiones de la Alta California, pp. 87-117.

Tate, V. D. "Spanish documents relating to the voyage of the Racoon to Astoria and San Francisco." HAHR, XVIII (1938), 184-191.

Taylor, A. S. Discovery of California and Northwest America. San Francisco, 1853. (19 p.)
Deals with the first voyage to the coasts of California, made in 1542 by Cabrillo and Ferrelo.

Tays, G. "California never was an independent republic." CHSQ, XV (1936), 242-243.

Tays, G. "The passing of Spanish California, September 29, 1822." CHSQ, XV (1936), 139-142.

Tays, G. "The surrender of Monterrey by Governor Nicolás Gutiérrez, November 5, 1836; an account from unpublished correspondence." CHSQ, XV (1936), 338-363.

Tays, G. "Captain Andrés Castillero, diplomat, an account from unpublished sources of his services to Mexico in the Alvarado revolution of 1836 - 1838." CHSQ, XIV (1935), 230-268.

Tays, G. (ed.). "Pío Pico's correspondence with the Mexican government, 1846 - 1848." CHSQ, XIII (1934), 99-149.

Tays, G. (trans.). "Record of Padre Fray Junípero Serra's death (1784) in the Book of the Dead of mission San Carlos at Carmel in the hand of Fray Francisco Palóu." CHSQ, XIII (1934), 155-158.

Teggart, F. J. (ed.). "The narrative of the Portolá expedition of 1769-1770, by Miguel Costansó." Berkeley: Academy of Pacific Coast History, Publications, I (1910), 91-159.

Teggart, F. J. (ed.). "The Portolá expedition of 1769-1770; diary of Miguel Costansó." Berkeley: Academy of Pacific Coast History, Publications,, II (1911), 161-327.

Teggart, F. J. (ed.). "The Anza expedition of 1775-1776; diary of Pedro Font." Berkeley: Academy of Pacific Coast History, Publications, III (1913), 1-131.

Temple, T. W. (ed.). "Lanterns at Monterey." CHSQ, XI (1932), 274-279.
    The description by Junípero Serra of the founding of Monterrey and of the first Corpus Christi celebration in Alta California, from his letter dated July 2, 1770.

Temple, T. W. "Soldiers and settlers of the expedition of 1781." Southern California Historical Society, Publications, XV (1933), pt. 1, 99-116.

Temple, T. W. "Se fundaron un pueblo de españoles." Southern California Historical Society, Publications, XV (1933), pt. 1, 69-98.
    Story of the founding of Los Angeles.

Thomas, A. B. "The Yellowstone river, James Long and Spanish reaction to American intrusion into Spanish dominions, 1818-1819." NMHR, IV (1929), 164-177.

Torchiana, H. A. van Coenen. The story of Mission Santa Cruz. San Francisco, 1933. (460 p.)

Upham, C. W. Life of John C. Fremont. Boston, 1856. (366 p.)

Van Brunt, J. California missions, painted and described. Los Angeles, 1940. (57 p.)

Vancouver, Capt. G. Voyage of discovery to the North Pacific Ocean and round the world . . . 1790-1795. 3 vols. London, 1798
    Numerous later and less accurate editions.

Wilbur, M. E. (trans. and ed). Juan Maria de Salvatierra, by Miguel Venegas. Cleveland, 1929. (350 p.)
    An excellent work with a brief biography of Salvatierra by the translator and editor. The translation was made from a rare copy of the biography of the Jesuit missionary by his confrere, Miguel Venegas.

Villaseñor y Villaseñor, A. Reclamaciones a Mexico por los fondos de California. Mexico, 1902. (272 p.)

Wagner, H. R. "The discovery of California." CHSQ, I (1922), 36-56.

Wagner, H. R. "Monterey in 1796." CHSQ, I (1922), 173-177.

Wagner, H. R. (ed.). "Unamuno's voyage to California in 1587." CHSQ, II (1923), 140-160.

Wagner, H. R. (trans. and ed.). "The voyage to California of Sabastián Rodríguez Cermeño in 1595." CHSQ, III (1924), 3-24.

Wagner, H. R. (ed.). "California voyages, 1539-1541." CHSQ, III (1924), 307-397.

Wagner, H. R. "Quivira, a mythical California city." CHSQ, III (1924), 262-267.

Wagner, H. R. "Some imaginary California geography." Worcester, Mass.: American Antiquarian Society, Proceedings, XXXVI (1926), pt. 1, 83-129.

Wagner, H. R. "Spanish voyages to the Northwest coast in the sixteenth century." CHSQ, VI (1927), 293-331; VII (1928), 20-77, 132-186, 228, 276, 295-394; VIII (1929), 26-70.

Wagner, H. R. Spanish voyages to the Northwest coast in the sixteenth century. San Francisco: California Historical Society, Publications, No. 4 (1929). (571 p.)
The series of studies edited in convenient book form.

Wagner, H. R. "A recently discovered account of the Atondo expedition to California in 1683." CHSQ, VIII (1929), p. 80.

Wagner, H. R. (trans.). "Pearl fishing enterprises in the Gulf of California; the expedition of Sebastián Vizcaíno." HAHR, X (1930), 188-220.
Translation of Vizcaíno's narrative, May 12, 1596, to December 8, 1596.

Wagner, H. R. "Apocryphal voyages to the Northwest coast." Worcester, Mass.: American Antiquarian Society. Proceedings, XLI (1931), 179-234.

Wagner, H. R. "The last Spanish exploration of the Northwest coast and the attempt to colonize Bodega Bay." CHSQ, X (1931), 313-345; also reprint, San Francisco; California Historical Society, 1931. (35 p.)

Wagner, H. R. (ed.). "A map of Cabrillo's discoveries." CHSQ, XI (1932), 44-46.

Wagner, H. R. "George Davidson, geographer of the Northwest coast of America." CHSQ, XI (1932), 299-320.

Wagner, H. R. (trans. and ed.). Spanish explorations in the strait of Juan de Fuca. Santa Ana, Calif., 1933. (323 p.)
Contains the Quimper expedition (1790), the Eliza expedition (1791), the Galieno-Valdés expedition (1792), and the establishment of the Spaniards at Neah Bay.

Wagner, H. R. (ed.). "Journal of Tomás de Suría of his voyage with Malaspina to the Northwest coast of America in 1791." PHR, V (1936), 234-276.

Wagner, H. R. (ed.). Letters of Captain Don Pedro Fages and the Reverend President Fr. Junípero Serra at San Diego, California, in October, 1772. San Francisco, 1937. (9 p.)
Facsimiles with English translation. In his introduction Wagner "concludes that Serra's suspicions of Fages were unjustified" (Hanke: Handbook, 1937, p. 289).

Wagner, H. R. (ed.). "Four early sketches of Monterrey scenes." CHSQ, XV (1936), 213-215.

Wagner, H. R. The cartography of the Northwest coast of America to the year 1800. 2 vols. Berkeley: University of California press, 1937. (270 and 271-543 p.)
This splendid work contains a wealth of material, the fruit of long years of intense research and study.

Wagner, H. R. Juan Rodríguez Cabrillo, discoverer of the coast of California. San Francisco: California Historical Society, 1941. (94 p.)

Walsh, M. T. The mission bells of California. San Francisco, 1934. (327 p.)

Waterman, I. R. Juan Rodríguez Cabrillo, discoverer of California. Sacramento: California State Printing Office, 1935. (22 p.)

Watson, D. S. (ed.). The Spanish occupation of California. San Francisco, 1934. (62 p.)

Assembles translations and studies prepared by others concerning the plan for establishing a government, the council held at San Blas on May 16, 1768, and the diary of expeditions made to California under the general leadership of Governor Portolá.

Watson, D. S. (ed.). The founding of the first California missions under the spiritual guidance of the Venerable Padre Fray Junípero Serra. San Francisco, 1934. (124 p.)

Contains "an historical account of the expeditions sent by land and sea in the year 1769, as told by Fray Francisco Palóu, and hitherto unpublished letters of Serra, Palóu, and Gálvez: the whole newly translated and arranged as a consecutive narrative, with the aid of Thomas W. Temple II, by Douglas S. Watson; to which is added the account of Serra's death inscribed by Fray Francisco Palóu in the book of the dead at Carmel mission" (subtitle).

Wilbur, M. E. Travels on the Pacific coast. 2 vols. Santa Ana, Calif., 1937.

Translation from the French of Duflot de Mofras's *Exploration du Territoire de L'Oregon, des Californies, et de la Mar Vermeille* . . . published in Paris in 1844.

Williams, M. F. "Mission, presidio and pueblo: notes on California local institutions under Spain and Mexico." CHSQ, I (1922), 23-35.

Williamson, J. A. "Drake's plate of brass." Geographic Journal (London), XCI (1928), 543-545.

Discusses the authenticity of the brass plate found in California and believed to be a relic of Drake's expedition.

Winsor, J. "Discoveries on the Pacific coast of North America." Narrative and Critical History of North America, II, 431-473.

Contains reproductions and explanations of contemporary charts.

Winther, O. O. "The story of San José, 1777-1869. CHSQ, XIV (1935). Also reprint, California Historical Society, Publications, No. 11 (1935). (54 p.)

Wright, I. A. (trans.). "Unamuno's voyage to California in 1587." CHSQ, II (1923), 140-160.

Wyllys, R. K. "French imperialists in California." CHSQ, VIII (1929), 116-129.

Visits of Frenchmen between 1830 and 1850, indicating French designs on Mexican possessions.

Cum Permissu Superiorum

Steck, Francis Borgia, 1884–
 A tentative guide to historical materials on the Spanish borderlands. New York, B. Franklin ₁1971₁

 1⁰⁶ p. 24 cm. (Burt Franklin research and source works series, 670. Geography and discovery, 12)

 Reprint of the 1943 ed.
 On spine: Guide to historical materials/Spanish borderlands.

 1. America—Discovery and exploration—Spanish—Bibliography. 2. Spain—Colonies — North America — Bibliography. 3. Southwest, New—History—Bibliography. 4. Southwest, Old—History—Bibliography. I. Title. II. Title: Guide to historical materials/Spanish borderlands.

285693 Z1251.S8S8 1971   016.976   71–143659
 ISBN 0–8337–33796   MARC

 Library of Congress   71 ₁4₁